A Paul to

Brinx/Kömmerling

A Paul to Kiss

Aus dem Deutschen
von David Fermer

Thienemann

Danger at Hand!

Mum is in love. No doubt about it. Everybody can tell, even if she won't **admit** it. She just says, "Rubbish! What makes you think that?" and turns red in the face. I repeat: red in the face!

We always eat breakfast together on Sundays. Every Sunday. The shop is closed and we have **plenty of** time to talk about **everything under the sun**. Mum owns a flower shop. Flowers and second-hand **junk**. Like old washstands with jugs inside, just in case someone decides to go without running water for a while and needs a jug to wash themselves with; or rusty window bars from Morocco, funny doorbell chains from Peru; or **butter-dishes** made out of **greaseproof paper** which has been hardened over thousands of years.

My dad's a banker: filthy rich, always stressed, constantly away from home. He's the kind of guy who disappears without a trace after your **concep-**

---

to admit – zugeben; plenty of – jede Menge;
everything under the sun – alles Mögliche; junk – Plunder;
butter-dish – Butterdose; greaseproof paper – Pergamentpapier

tion. Which is what he did. With all his money. And we **reckon** we're lucky he did.

I put two slices of bread into the toaster – my **good deed** for the day – while Mum cuts small figures out of the butter with rusty **moulds** from Tyrol.

"By the way, I won't be at home this evening," she says **casually** and smiles that dreamy, euphoric smile which she always has when she's in love. This is something that happens every now and again, but it's usually over before I know it. I don't get worked up about it. I only wish she'd just admit it!

"Are you going out with an old friend of yours? Some woman I've never met?" I **pull her leg** and toss the golden brown toast elegantly onto her plate.

"I'm going out with a man," she snaps back at me and melts the Tyrolean butter pig on her warm slice of toast.

I know that she'll never eat that slice of toast. She's simply too much in love. She's busy looking **dreamily** into the air. And what's more, when she gets up, she'll knock her chair over, making her jump, and the stack of dishes, which she's about to

---

conception – Zeugung; to reckon – meinen;
a good deed – eine gute Tat; mould – Ausstecher;
casual – beiläufig/lässig; to pull sb's leg – jmdn. aufziehen;
dreamy – verträumt/versonnen

carry over to the sink, will crash to the floor and **shatter** into all four corners of the kitchen. But it's OK. Mum's in love. It doesn't matter if both her eyes are looking in different directions.

"Are you going to the **flea market** with ABC today?" she asks, spreading the butter on her slice of toast.

"Sure thing! It's the second Sunday of the month!" That means the flea market is at the main square. A quality **range of goods**. Anna, Babsi, Carla – ABC, got it? – and I never miss it. "What are you up to then, you and your boyfriend?"

"Oh, come on, Olivia, stop **being** such **a pain**. Just drop it, will you?" She only ever says Olivia when she's deadly serious. **Otherwise,** I'm known as Olli.

"Going to the cinema to hold hands?"

"Unlike you, my dear, we're not thirteen anymore!" Mum snaps at me, and I decide it would be better to go now before the **aforementioned** dishes crash to the floor and I have to **redecorate** the kitchen.

"Am I going to see you later?" Mum shouts after me and I already know the answer: before she goes

---

to shatter – zerbrechen; flea market – Flohmarkt/Trödelmarkt; range of goods – Warenangebot;
to be a pain – einem auf die Nerven gehen; otherwise – sonst; aforementioned – oben erwähnt; to redecorate – renovieren

out, she'll come crawling to me to ask which **hairdo** and dress I think **suit** her best. You know, the whole **shebang**. It's always the same, and there's absolutely **no point** to it all. It's a mystery to me why Mum doesn't have any luck with men. She's a great person. She looks good for her age, she's hardly got any **wrinkles** (she's just a bit **tubby** around the **waist**, but the fat slips easily into her underpants), and her breasts are in good shape. Maybe she's just forgotten how it works with the opposite sex. No idea. But it's all the same to me, honest. I can't be bothered with some guy who wants to **butt in** on our wonderful life and **mess** everything **up**.

You see, during the week Mum works in the shop and I have the place to myself. ABC come around and we do everything together. Shopping, cooking, hanging out – whatever we fancy really. So no, we don't want anyone messing that up for us. No way! He might think Mum's too easy-going and ought to be **stricter** or something like that. No one can possibly understand how we live – and they don't need to either! I want everything to stay just as it is. And the girls think exactly the same.

---

hairdo – Frisur; to suit sb (clothes) – jmdm. stehen;
shebang – Drum und Dran; no point – kein Zweck/Sinn;
wrinkle – Falte; tubby – pummelig; waist – Taille;
to butt in – dazwischenplatzen;
to mess sth up – etw. verpfuschen; strict – streng

As I put on my coat and search through the drawers for money, I hear something go bang in the kitchen – the chair! And then something smashes – the dishes! Oh well, looks like I'll have to keep my eyes open for a few old cups at the flea market. **Replacement** cups, so to speak.

Before I go, I give Mum a kiss. She's **sweeping up** the broken dishes and seems to be in a good mood, although she has absolutely no idea how this could have happened again.

"Perhaps because of your old friend," I suggest.

She sticks out her tongue at me, just to be on the safe side, in case I'm pulling her leg. But I'm not. Word of honour from Miss Crossed-Fingers!

ABC are sitting on a **fence** like chickens **in a roost**. They're waiting for me near the snack bar at the entrance to the flea market. Well, Babsi and Carla are sitting. Anna would never sit on a fence.

"**It's not the done thing**," she claims.

Carla sets about tearing her to pieces. "And why not?"

"Girls don't sit on fences."

"Says who?"

"Says me."

---

replacement – Ersatz-; to sweep up – fegen;
fence – Zaun; in a roost – auf der Stange;
it's not the done thing – das macht man nicht

"What a load of rubbish! Your mum might say that, or the Almighty Book of Morals, or old men, or Islamists. But not you! You don't really think that!"

Anna always tries to make a really **respectable** impression, but no one ever buys it. At least, not us. And least of all Carla.

Babsi interrupts the two of them because she knows this could **degenerate into** a debate that goes on for hours. "Let's get out of here. Chorche's coming!"

Jorge is from South America, which means his name is **pronounced** *Chorche*. And no one can pronounce it with more contempt – and can dig the name out of the back of her throat better – than Babsi. She can usually find at least one reasonable quality about every boy she sees, but Jorge is just too **pushy**. He's so in love with her, he's constantly running after her.

"Where did his Argentinian pride get to?" snorts Babsi and we **scram**.

"Isn't he from Chile?" asks Anna.

But you can tell by the way nobody answers her question that we just don't care.

---

respectable – anständig;
to degenerate into sth – in etw. ausarten;
to pronounce – aussprechen; pushy – aufdringlich;
to scram – abhauen

Babsi disappears off to the nearest make-up stall to look for some new lipstick and stay **on the run** from Jorge.

"Look at those cups!" I exclaim excitedly. I've spotted a bright orange **mother-of-pearl** Turkish tea service. Far out!

"It's a knockout!" Anna.

"It's **awful**!" Carla. She thinks nearly everything is awful. That's just the way she is. But because she's also incredibly **well read** and knows all about 'life, the world and the universe', she can always explain things to you. As long as you think everything is awful as well.

"I don't want to know!" I interrupt. I'm not interested in her opinion. I just want to know how much it costs.

"Forty!" replies the man.

I put on a face of absolute horror. "Forty euros for four cups?"

"And **saucers**," points out the man.

"Five euros, that's my final offer!" And I haven't got more to offer anyway.

"You can't waste five euros on kitsch like that!" Carla is **gobsmacked**.

"But they cost forty euros. The man just said,"

---

on the run – auf der Flucht; mother-of-pearl – Perlmutt;
awful – furchtbar; well read – belesen;
saucer – Untertasse; gobsmacked – baff

butts in Anna. Thank you, Anna, that was quite unnecessary. Things like that can ruin **negotiations**.

"That's right!" agrees the man. I could have guessed!

OK. No mother-of-pearl cups then.

Babsi turns up with bright red lips. She has a rather large mouth and is really proud of it. "**Wicked**, huh?" she asks us, **wiggling** her bottom and licking her lips like Marilyn Monroe. She likes to model herself on Monroe. Only she doesn't want to die quite so young.

"**Revolting**," says Carla, but this doesn't bother Babsi because Carla thinks everything is revolting. "Do you know how many monkeys have been subjected to an **agonising** death just so you can **get all dolled up**?"

"A hundred? Two hundred? I've really no idea, Carla!" answers Babsi sarcastically, not letting herself get **wound up**.

"Don't you think it's a bit too red?" asks Anna. "What are the boys going to think?"

"That I'm sexy and they all want to kiss me!" sighs Babsi. Then she gives Anna a quick kiss, leaving her a huge lipstick print on her **cheek**.

---

negotiation – Verhandlung; wicked – verrucht/geil;
to wiggle – wackeln; revolting – ekelhaft; agonising – qualvoll;
to get all dolled up – sich aufbrezeln;
to wind sb up – jmdn. aufziehen; cheek – Wange

"I see what you mean, Babsi. It works," I say with a grin because I can see Jorge has spotted us and is heading towards Babsi.

We have to get out of here quickly. It's easy enough to disappear between all the stalls, and we soon manage to lose him.

"What's that?" I spot something between a brand new soda siphon, a shower head and four hundred old CDs. It's a kind of camera. I turn it over in my hands and take a look through the **viewfinder**.

"It's a Super 8 camera. They were on the market before video. It takes really small, thin film." Carla is informed, of course.

I **flip out**. "We can buy it and make a film!"

"I'll take the role of the happily married **landowner's** wife!" cries Anna.

Carla rolls her eyes. "What if there's no landowner's wife in the film?"

"Olli, there can be a landowner's wife, can't there? Her husband comes home from the cotton fields on his horse every day and ..." **gushes** Anna.

"... he's tired because he spent the whole day whipping his slaves and forcing them to work for no money." Carla. Who else?

---

viewfinder – Sucher; to flip out – ausflippen;
landowner – Gutsbesitzer;
to gush – etwas schwärmerisch sagen

Babsi wants to play Monroe, of course. "I wanna be loved by you …!" she sings, slinging a **fluffy** boa over her shoulder which she found under a **screw-driver** set.

"Our slaves are paid!" proclaims Anna.

"Sounds like a great movie!" sighs Carla.

"How about buying the camera first?" I suggest quietly. "Maybe it costs a million euros, and then we can forget the whole thing."

But it costs eight euros. After tough negotiations. We all **chip in**. After all, we're going into the movie business together – ABC and O. All or none.

After that I only see the world around me through the viewfinder of the camera. There's no film in it though. Of course, the salesman only mentioned that the film is incredibly expensive – because Super 8 hardly exists anymore – after we'd dug deep into our pockets and paid him. But so what? Then we'll just shoot short films, for special occasions. At the moment I can see various parts of my mother's body in the viewfinder, depending on where I **pan**. She's trying to **do herself up** as best she can, but she's completely beside herself with despair because she has nothing to wear. I zoom in

---

fluffy – flauschig; screwdriver – Schraubenzieher;
to chip in – beisteuern; to pan – hinschwenken;
to do oneself up – sich zurechtmachen

to the pile of clothes which has already been torn out of the wardrobe. Why is it always the same old story? In every film, every book, and in real life, whenever someone is in love and has a date with their victim, panic breaks out about what they're going to wear. Why don't people just go as they are? As soon as they get to know each other a bit better, they go back to wearing their old baggy pullovers anyway – the ones that make them look like they **weigh** a few tonnes, but are really rather comfortable.

"The red one? What do you think?" Mum holds up a **skintight** dress to me. "Just put that damn thing down, will you, Olli?"

OK, I can see I'm going to have to concentrate here. I put the camera down. "I think you look best in your jeans."

"Oh, come on, I can't wear them."

"Yes, you can. And then go smart on top – a tight T-shirt and blazer."

Mum looks hesitant – maybe I'm right. She **delves** into her wardrobe and I rock backwards and forwards in her wickerwork **rocking chair**. I bet that looks good through the camera: the picture moving up and down, up and down, up and down …

---

to weigh – wiegen; skintight – hauteng; to delve – kramen; rocking chair – Schaukelstuhl

"Maybe a more casual look is a good idea. Robert works at a **youth centre**. Perhaps he prefers the casual type anyway!"

Robert! In **tender** moments known as Bob. Or Bobby? I think I'm going to **puke**! I hope he stays away from here! But Mum's looking pretty damn hot now. And it was me who gave her the tip.

"Although, if I worked at a youth centre," I suggest in the hope of getting her to change her mind, "I'd probably wear a baggy pullover." No chance.

Now I just have to help her **curl her hair**. About a hundred hours later she's all set to leave.

"Bye, sweetheart. Thanks a lot!" A kiss on the cheek for Olli, whose fault it will be if Robert can't **resist** her. "By the way, I think there's a projector in the **storeroom**."

A projector! A Super 8 projector? And she only mentions that now?

The storeroom is in the **attic**. There's a staircase leading to it directly from our flat. You just have to open the trapdoor and then you're in **Junk** Paradise. Mum can't throw anything away, and some people claim I've inherited this from her. But it's a bit different with me. Sure thing, I love junk of any kind.

---

youth centre – Jugendzentrum; tender – zärtlich;
to puke – kotzen; to curl one's hair – sich Locken drehen;
to resist – widerstehen; storeroom – Lagerraum;
attic – Dachboden; junk – Trödel/Kram

That's why I'm always hanging out at flea markets. But whereas my mum collects everything and puts it in the storeroom, I **do up** the things I find and see what I can make out of them. I like things that are broken most of all, things that no one else wants. I **amass** them in my room until I can think of a way to breathe life back into them. Then they have to get used to having a different purpose. Like instead of being a record player with no pick-up arm, they're a fantastic **rotating cake stand**.

I spend the rest of the evening partly in the storeroom looking for the projector and partly in the kitchen cleaning it up. Unbelievable. Now all we need is a roll of film which I plan to buy in the morning.

It looks like Robert is a very entertaining guy. Mum doesn't come home. At all. At least not before I fall asleep.

When I wake up it's the middle of the night and I **need a pee**. I shuffle over to the toilet. I don't turn on the lights because I don't want to wake up Mum. I'm sitting there on the toilet with the door wide open (after all, why should I shut it in the middle of the night?), and I can **barely** keep my eyes open,

---

to do up sth – etw. aufpolieren/aufmöbeln;
to amass – anhäufen;
rotating cake stand – rotierender Kuchenpräsentierteller;
to need a pee – aufs Klo müssen; barely – kaum

when someone turns on the toilet light from outside.

"Hey, turn it off!" I groan, thinking it's Mum.

But all of a sudden, I see a tall, hairy man standing in front of me wearing his boxer shorts **back to front**.

"Hey, what are you doing?" I shout and slam the door in his face.

The hairy monkey – I'd put my money on him being Robert – nearly jumps out of his skin. He quickly turns off the light, leaving me in a state of shock in the dark. It's never gone this far before. Mum's never brought anyone home with her. And she certainly hasn't let them get undressed. This is serious. More serious than ever before. Deadly serious! There's an unbelievably hairy danger at hand – a threat to my very existence – right in front of the toilet door!

---

back to front – verkehrt herum

𝒜 Gorilla and Freckles

It's dark. Not because it's night, but because the **undergrowth** surrounding me is so dense that I can't even make out the faintest shimmer of light. I **painstakingly** cut my way through the undergrowth with my machete. Progress is slow and I have nothing on my feet. I try not to look down. I don't want to see the **creepy-crawlies** scuttling around on the ground. But even though I don't look down, I can still see them: the spiders, the worms, the **leeches**, oozing over the slimy ground, my feet right in the middle of them. I have to be careful of the **creepers**. They're creeping around my neck, squeezing me tight, for no apparent reason, just because, even though they won't be able to eat me afterwards. They don't have any mouths. I use all my strength to beat a path through the undergrowth, and after yet another swing I bump into something big, black and furry. It blocks my path. It seems to

---

freckles – Sommersprossen;
undergrowth – Gestrüpp/Unterholz; painstaking – mühsam;
creepy-crawly – Krabbeltier; leech – Blutegel;
creeper – Schlingpflanze

be everywhere. I glance up and find myself looking straight into the **ugly mug** of a gorilla. His mouth isn't big enough to hide the metre-long fangs protruding from his upper jaw. That might explain why he's **dribbling** so badly. That and the fact that his mouth starts watering upon seeing me. I turn around. I have to go back, to get out of here. Escape! But the creepers creep up from behind and the gorilla **looms** in front, and there's no way out through the undergrowth to the side. And the gorilla is wearing a pair of boxer shorts …

"Olli, sweetheart, time to wake up! What's the matter?" The gorilla is wearing boxer shorts and talks like my mother?

I open my eyes and find myself lying in bed. I don't know how I made it back here last night.

First of all I spent an **eternity** sitting on the toilet, trying to digest what I'd just seen and trying to find a solution. How do you **chase off** a gorilla? But I couldn't come up with any good ideas, and then I wanted to call ABC. At three o'clock in the morning? – **That's not on**! So I went back to bed, as quiet as a mouse, hoping that the Hairy One wouldn't shoot out from some hidden corner.

Mum strokes my sweaty nightmare hair, with

---

ugly mug – Fratze; to dribble – sabbern; to loom – aufragen; eternity – Ewigkeit; to chase off – verjagen; That's not on! – Das ist nicht erlaubt!

the same hand that she used to take off Robert's underpants. "Were you dreaming about the man you bumped into last night?" she asks with a smile, but I really can't see what there is to smile about.

"Man? I bumped into a gorilla!" I sit up in bed and bring the act of motherly tenderness to an end.

Mum laughs and looks dreamily into the distance. "You're right. Robert's hairy all over. Sweet, don't you think?"

Oh my God. She's gone blind! Completely **off her rocker**. Out of her mind. Sweet? No man has ever been sweet before. Let alone a gorilla! "OK, Mum, tell me the truth: how much time have I got?"

Mum has no idea what I'm talking about.

"How much time have I got before you marry the sweet gorilla and I have to look for another place to live?"

Mum gets to her feet irritably and heads towards the door, **steering clear** of the conversation. "Now **cut it out**!"

What's that supposed to mean? Why does she come up with something stupid like that? Cut what out? Eh?

---

to be off one's rocker – nicht mehr alle Tassen im Schrank haben; to steer clear of sth – etw. meiden;
Cut it out! – Mach mal halblang!

"Just because Robert spent the night here, doesn't mean a thing!"

"He had his underpants on back to front!"

"So what? What's that supposed to mean?"

Don't be like that, Mum! "It means that he took them off **beforehand**. And because he had to go for a pee and is a respectable gorilla, he put them on back to front in the dark." I'm just glad he was wearing them at all! What a thought …!

Mum shakes her head and leaves the room muttering, "You're **getting ideas into your head**!"

But it's **proof. Infallible** proof. We've often talked about Mum's boyfriends together. She was always really enthusiastic after the first date. And this time? She's playing it down! She's **putting a downer on** it! It's a clear-cut case for me: there's danger ahead! This gorilla could be around for a while, and I have to talk to the others urgently. Quick!

When there's something we need to talk about urgently, we do the toilet routine. ABC go to school on the bus, and I go on foot. Babsi is usually late because she needs so long in the bathroom in the

---

beforehand – vorher;
to get ideas into one's head – sich etw. einreden;
proof – Beweis; infallible – unfehlbar/absolut;
to put a downer on sth – etw. herunterspielen

morning. So we have no alternative but to discuss matters during class time once all of us are there. The toilet routine is really simple: one after the other each of us tells the teacher that we have to go to the toilet. And then we do just that.

Of course, there are teachers who get **suspicious**, and there are others who try to stop us from leaving. "Carla, I just can't believe that you also have to go to the toilet right now. You can't **fool** me!" barks Mr Schrödinger, for instance.

But then Carla just starts **unbuttoning** her trousers. "Then I'll just have to go to the toilet here," she mumbles, and the teacher changes his mind – in a flash.

"Do you think she's really in love?" asks Anna in wonder from inside her **cubicle**.

"Why not? It happens to me all the time," says Babsi from another.

"I bet the guy's just using her. Who else would **get taken in** by a gorilla?" Carla from cubicle number three.

We always sit in different cubicles, just in case a suspicious teacher comes to take a look.

---

suspicious – misstrauisch;
to fool sb – jmdn. zum Narren halten;
to unbutton – aufknöpfen; cubicle – Klokabine;
to get taken in – sich hereinlegen lassen

"The facts of the case are as follows," I explain again. "First of all, my mum is **all over the place** ..."

"You always are when you fall in love," points out Babsi.

"Exactly! And secondly, the guy spent the night at our place, and he had his underpants on back to front!"

"That's really **gross**!" squeals Anna.

"And thirdly, she **denies** that it's serious."

"This really is a dramatic situation!" concludes Carla.

Babsi comes out of her cubicle to **touch up** her lipstick. She's always doing that: in front of shop windows, in the middle of class with the aid of her auntie-like pocket mirror, before a meal, after a meal and during a meal. "**For crying out loud**, what are you all getting so worked up about? Olli's mum isn't a **nun**."

I rush out of my cubicle and try to make it perfectly clear to her. "What if it really *is* serious? And I'm convinced it is. No doubt about it. The day after tomorrow the gorilla will be living at our place, **throwing his weight around**. That means that having the place to ourselves every afternoon

---

to be all over the place – durch den Wind sein; gross – ekelhaft; to deny – leugnen; to touch up – etw. auffrischen; For crying out loud! – Um Himmels willen!; nun – Nonne; to throw your weight around – seinen Einfluss geltend machen

is history. Freedom is history. Do you know what I'm talking about? Guys like that suddenly start feeling responsible for you. It happens in a flash. He works at some youth centre as well. He thinks he knows what he's doing!"

Carla and Anna join us.

Anna puts her arm around my shoulder and tries to calm me down. "You'll get used to it. Just think if they got married! The four of us as **bridesmaids**, all in silk and flowers …"

"Anna!" Carla looks grimly through her glasses into nothingness, as if she could see the future there. "Olli's right. It's a disaster and could mean the end of the good life for all of us."

Just as Carla is saying this, the teacher comes in, **catching** us **red-handed**, delighted at doing so. He smiles from ear to ear. "Got you, you *baggage*!" It's the French teacher, no doubt about it.

But we don't let anybody walk over us. No way.

Anna puts on her look of horror. When she does that she looks like she's just about to have a heart attack and the only thing you want to do is stroke her head. "Oh, that's awful. I'm so sorry. I didn't mean to upset you!"

Babsi toys with the top button of her blouse. She smiles at the teacher and swings her hips in perfect

---

bridesmaid – Brautjungfer;
to catch sb red-handed – jmdn. auf frischer Tat ertappen

Marilyn Monroe style, fluttering her eyelids slightly. "It was pure coincidence, us meeting here!" she says with a beaming smile. "Honest!"

Carla folds her arms over her chest and gives me a nod: I'm meant to follow her. We walk past the teacher with our heads held high. "I don't know what you're doing here in the girls' toilets, Monsieur Schrödinger. As far as we're concerned, we're going to class." Then she turns to me. "Shall we **refrain from** reporting him for the **harassment** of **underage** girls, Olivia?"

"We'll have to think about that, won't we?" I say.

We all nod and **strut** past Schrödinger, and his mouth just hangs open. There's nothing to smile about anymore.

No one can walk over us that easily. Certainly not Carla. After all, she's convinced that the world is going to end tomorrow anyway. So what's she got to lose?

We have to **postpone** the meeting until the afternoon at my place. On the way home I pop into a photo shop to buy a film. A Super 8 film! We've **scraped together** every last cent we have. But we haven't talked about what we want to film yet.

---

to refrain from doing sth – von etw. absehen;
harassment – Belästigung; underage – minderjährig;
to strut – stolzieren; to postpone – verschieben;
to scrape together – zusammenkratzen

The man in the photo shop is really **chuffed** because no one's come to buy a Super 8 film for over a hundred years. He quickly shows me how to put the cartridge in, **talking nineteen to the dozen,** and even knocks two euros off the price because it's been lying around the shop for over a hundred years anyway. "Which doesn't **affect** its quality, don't you worry, young lady!"

No, don't you worry, young man, I'm not worried!

As I come out of the shop I observe the world through the camera's viewfinder. I slowly pan down the street: a little bus shelter, a tramp, streetlamps, a dustbin, a bicycle stand – wait a sec, back to the dustbin. Someone has thrown away an umbrella. That's ridiculous! Just because the cover has **got into** a bit of **a tangle**. There's a button on the camera to enlarge the picture. Zoom! That's just what I do. The umbrella is **in perfect condition.** You could make a … a … wonderful photo stand out of it, for instance. Take off the covering and then clip the photos to the wires with **clothes pegs.** That's a good idea. I start heading over to the dust-

---

to be chuffed about sth – sich über etw. freuen;
to talk nineteen to the dozen – reden wie ein Wasserfall;
to affect sth – eine Auswirkung auf etw. haben;
to get into a tangle – sich verheddern;
in perfect condition – in tadellosem Zustand;
clothes peg – Wäscheklammer

bin, the camera to my eye and the umbrella in sight, but just before I get there – I've only knocked over four pedestrians on the way – someone else grabs the umbrella. I **shrink back**. It can't be!

Zoom out. Wide shot. The whole picture. Some guy who's about the same age as me, maybe a bit older, is examining the umbrella in detail, opening and closing it at will.

Zoom in. Close up of the face. He's quite **cute**. Unbelievably cute in fact. No doubt about it. He's **gorgeous**. It must **be down to** his million freckles – but he doesn't have red hair. His hair is all **straggly**. I'm captivated by the look in his eyes: he's really concentrating. It looks like he's thinking about what he could make with the umbrella. Just like I just did. And it looks like he's come up with an idea. Anyhow, he takes the umbrella with him, and I press the *film* button. I follow him. He's so cute I don't let him out of my sight. I have to admit: it's not because of the umbrella.

I walk slowly behind him, filming his each and every move: the way he says hello to some other guys who he seems to know; the way he **dangles** the umbrella in his hand and a black musical in-

---

to shrink back – zurückweichen; cute – hübsch/süß;
gorgeous – sehr attraktiv;
to be down to sth – mit etw. zusammenhängen;
straggly – zottelig/zerzaust; to dangle – baumeln lassen

strument case in the other; the way he goes down into the underground, gets onto **the tube** and disappears.

Then the film **runs out** – it only lasts three minutes, this ridiculously expensive strip of celluloid – and the boy with the freckles is gone.

---

the tube – die U-Bahn; to run out – ausgehen

ABC on the Bus

"Olli is in love. It's as clear as day. I just have a **gut feeling** for things like this!" Babsi is sitting on the left of the back seat of the bus.

"Just because she spent all yesterday afternoon talking about this **supposedly** great guy?" says Carla from the right.

Anna sits in the middle, looking from one to the other and along the long aisle to the bus driver.

Babsi leans across Anna to Carla. "Well, I've never known Olli like this. Have you ever heard her talking about a boy like this before? Have you ever seen her eyes light up like that? And that dreamy look in her eyes? Have you ever seen Olli like that?"

Carla **shrugs her shoulders**. "Maybe with Lubo. But anyway, **there's something funny going on**. First her mum, then her … I tell you, there's something **rotten** in the Pohlmann family."

"She used up all of our film," butts in Anna, vis-

---

gut feeling – instinktives Gefühl; supposedly – angeblich;
to shrug one's shoulders – mit den Achseln zucken;
There's something funny going on! – Da stimmt was nicht!;
rotten – faul

ibly unhappy about this fact. And when Anna is visibly unhappy about something, her eyes suddenly look like those of a cocker spaniel, her bottom lip wobbles slightly and her forehead **creases up** into four thousand wrinkles. "So much for the landowner's wife!"

"You wouldn't have got a **part** anyway, Miss Wobbly Lip!" growls Carla **scornfully**.

"Besides, any of us would have done the same," Babsi tries to **placate** Anna. "Imagine you bumped into your **Prince Charming**, and you just happened to have a camera with you. For crying out loud, even you'd start filming!"

"I wouldn't know where the button was."

Carla groans and Babsi continues to explain, "And it means she now has the possibility of showing us her Prince Charming – the only possibility. That's great: a real document. It's hard **evidence** that the guy even exists! How often have we thought 'There he is, my Prince Charming', and – whoosh – it turns out it isn't him at all!"

"Never happened to me!" says Carla.

"Just imagine …" mumbles Anna, lost in thought.

"What?" ask Babsi and Carla, although neither of them really wants to know.

---

to crease sth up – etw. zerknittern; part – Rolle; scornful – verächtlich; to placate sb – jmdn. beruhigen; Prince Charming – Märchenprinz; evidence – Beweis

"Just imagine he really is a prince, like Charles and Lady Di back then." Anna flutters her eyelids dreamily down the central aisle.

Babsi and Carla turn their heads, one to the right, one to the left, and look out of the window, ever so slightly **exasperated**. But only slightly.

"Overnight hordes of photographers would follow Olli wherever she went, and the prince would give her a diadem, and she'd have to buy loads of new clothes from Chanel and Versace. **Needless to say**, he'd pay. I mean, it's not her fault he's a real prince and as his wife she has to wear expensive clothes on official visits."

No one says a thing. **At a loss for words**.

Anna sighs. "And after she's worn everything once, she can pass them on to her best friends."

Carla makes a sound like a horse and scrapes her hooves.

Babsi **pats** Anna on the back of her head. "Dream on, girl! Anyway, I'm really looking forward to seeing the film. Aren't you, Carla?"

Carla **waves her hand dismissively**. "Prince Charmings all look the same."

---

exasperated – verärgert;
needless to say – selbstverständlich;
to be at a loss for words – um Worte verlegen sein;
to pat – leicht klopfen;
to wave one's hand dismissively – abwinken

“Maybe not Prince Charmings with broken umbrellas!” says Babsi with a grin.

The bus comes to a standstill and Jorge gets on.

“Oh no, it’s Chorche!” shrieks Anna.

Jorge sways down the central aisle towards Anna. He knows perfectly well how good-looking he is.

“What are we going to do now? He’s coming over!” whispers Anna to her friends.

But they’ve already taken cover behind the seats in front of them, and Anna is left to face the horror all alone, whether she likes it or not.

Looking for HIM

At last! The film is ready.

Today I'm going to show HIM to the girls. HIM, whose name I don't even know. HIM, who I spotted in the middle of the street. I've only ever seen him once – one time only. I haven't seen him since. HE, the boy who apparently only ever came to this area once **by coincidence**.

At first I thought, OK, he's a cute-looking guy, I've seen him now and … and – now **I just can't get him out of my mind**.

"Oh, come on, you're just imagining things," Babsi had claimed. "It's like when you really want to have an expensive jacket, but you can't get it: you think about it day and night until you see the next, even more expensive jacket hanging in the shop window."

Maybe that's what Babsi's like, but not me. I've never really had a lot to do with boys. Except for the ones trying to date Mum. And then it's always

---

by coincidence – zufällig;
I can't get sth/sb out of my mind – etw./jmd. will mir einfach nicht mehr aus dem Kopf gehen

been a **hassle**. Yeah, and with Lubo, **fair enough**, but that doesn't count.

Lubo goes to our school. He's two classes above us, and he's unbelievably good-looking. Good-looking, cool and **unapproachable**. He's the school rebel, if there is such a thing. The trendsetter. The guy who does everything differently. Like he was the first person to wear his jacket inside out, the first person to go barefoot in winter (either because he wanted to see if he could **hack** it, or to demonstrate for people in **Chechnya** who had to hack it as well, whether they wanted to or not), and he was the first person who played his guitar for the entire **break**. And when he plays, his long hair falls into his face. And when the teacher on duty comes up to him and tells him that break is over, Lubo is by no means of the same opinion. Everybody is in love with Lubo. Everybody wants to kiss Lubo. Everybody **apart from** Carla, of course. But he's untouchable. He's **light years** away. You can be in love with him, but not a lot more. That's why Lubo doesn't really count. And that's why HE is the first boy I've been thinking about 24 hours a day, even though I don't know anything about him. I've only

---

hassle – Ärger; fair enough – na schön/o.k.;
unapproachable – unnahbar; to hack sth – etw. aushalten;
Chechnya – Tschetschenien; break – Pause;
apart from – außer; light year – Lichtjahr

really seen him once for three minutes, through the lens of a prehistoric Super 8 camera. That's why I'm really excited now because I'm about to see him again – only on film. But that's better than nothing.

We've met up at my place after school and set up a little cinema in my bedroom. I'm **responsible** for the projector. It's not that easy. First of all you have to position it accurately so that the beam of light fits into the space which you've made by taking down just one of the many posters. To do that you need: a chair, three telephone books, the Bible – because we don't have a fourth telephone book – and three to four thin paperbacks for fine **adjustments**. You put the projector on top of that. Then you have to **thread in the film**. Inside there are about four million reels and spools and loops and **cogs**, and the film has to run all the way through. It's designed like that, so that only the Cleverest of the Clever can become projectionists. Like me, ha, ha!

After successfully making celluloid salad three times and having to cut off ten centimetres of film – oh, what an awful waste of unseen, freckled material – I **pull** it **off**.

Anna lays out the cushions and comfy **blankets**

---

responsible – zuständig; adjustment – Einstellung;
to thread in the film – den Film einlegen; cog – Zahnrad;
to pull sth off – etw. schaffen; blanket – Decke

for the audience to sit on, meaning us. Babsi brings the entire contents of the fridge into my bedroom and decorates a plate with **mouth-watering** sour cherries, olives, slices of ham and a half-eaten piece of Camembert. Carla is responsible for making the room dark. She's standing at the window, ready to draw the curtains at the right moment. And as ever she's also responsible for trying to put me in a bad mood. "What happened to the gorilla? I haven't heard anything about him since Prince Charming turned up."

I run the projector for a bit, rattling the film backwards and forwards. What right has the gorilla to be here now?! Of all times! "I think things have settled down. It was a **storm in a teacup**."

It's true that I haven't seen him since that awful creepy-toilet-night, and Mum has been behaving quite normally again. At least I think so. But I haven't really paid much attention to her. Because of him, Prince Charming, as Carla calls him. My thoughts are elsewhere, simple as that.

"When's it starting? I can't wait!" Anna throws herself onto the cushions and slips olives and sour cherries **alternately** into her mouth.

"OK. We can start," I give the go-ahead.

---

mouth-watering – appetitlich; a storm in a teacup – viel Aufregung umsonst, (sinngemäß:) Sturm im Wasserglas; alternate – abwechselnd

Carla draws the curtains and leans against the wall with her arms folded over her chest. Typical. She doesn't make herself comfortable because she's too busy demonstrating her **disapproval**.

"Are you ready?" I ask the group theatrically. "Ready for the best-looking guy you've ever seen?"

"We're ready!" cry Anna and Babsi.

"We'll see," mumbles Carla.

I start the projector running, and it rattles for the next three minutes. Nobody says a word. We stare spellbound at the jolting pictures on the wall and the sweet guy who is walking around in them. He's even cuter than I remember. He's unbelievable. I just have to find out his name, where he lives and what he's like. I have to see him again. And that has nothing to do with expensive or even more expensive coats!

After the underground train moves off in the film, I turn on the light and look **full of expectation** into my friends' faces. "So? What do you say?"

"I wouldn't kick him out of bed!" says Babsi with an **acknowledging** nod. "If you **go off** him, you can **turn to me with complete confidence**."

---

disapproval – Missbilligung; full of expectation – gespannt; acknowledging – anerkennend;
to go off sb – jmdn. nicht mehr mögen; to turn to sb with complete confidence – sich vertrauensvoll an jmdn. wenden

"He's gorgeous – **drop-dead** gorgeous," sighs Anna, putting on her rapturous face. That's when her eyes go all **blurry**, she **puckers her lips**, and you get the feeling she's about to burst into tears any second. "You have to find him, Olli. He's your dream guy. If you don't see him again, you might as well become a nun! You suit each other really well!"

"You can't say that," growls Carla. She hasn't given up her disapproving **stance**. Still: if you know her, you can spot a touch of **admiration** in her face. I'm sure about that.

"But how am I supposed to find him? I have no clues at all, and he hasn't come back to the photo shop since then."

"Have you got any **nail polish remover**?" Babsi scrutinises her fingernails which are flaking slightly. She can think best while she does her pedicure.

But, of course, I don't have the right equipment for that.

"It's really difficult!" Anna tugs at her blond curls, twisting them into a pigtail, and she then ties them into a knot so that her hair doesn't fall into her face while she's thinking.

---

drop-dead – absolut; blurry – verschwommen;
to pucker one's lips – die Lippen spitzen;
stance – Stand[punkt]; admiration – Bewunderung;
nail polish remover – Nagellack-Entferner

"It's not difficult at all!" Carla pushes herself off the wall and sits down next to us. "There were loads of **clues** in the film." You can always **rely on** Carla in situations like this. She's eagle-eyed, she doesn't miss a thing – not even the smallest detail – and she's smart.

"What were they?" I can't wait to find out.

Carla goes over to the projector, rewinds the film and runs it from the start – needless to say, she can do it just like that. Why did I need so much time?

"Here. What's he got in his hand?"

"A musical instrument case," I answer.

"Right. To be more precise, a **trumpet** case. So the guy plays the trumpet. There probably aren't that many guys in town who do that. You could go around all the trumpet teachers and music schools. For example. And look here: he obviously knows these guys."

"So what? How does that help me?"

Carla stops the film. "They've all got skateboards with them. You know, typical boys."

"Yes, but not my one!" I quickly **object**. I don't want Carla to talk badly about HIM.

"Not YOUR one," replies Carla dryly. "But he knows them, and you could ask around the skateboard gangs. For example."

---

clue – Hinweis; to rely on sb – sich auf jmdn. verlassen; trumpet – Trompete; to object – einwenden

Not a bad idea. Not at all a bad idea.

"And here you can see which train he's getting onto: the U3 towards the town centre. You could check out this tube station at around the same time of day and see if he gets on. Maybe he uses it often. Maybe his trumpet teacher is in the town centre, or he lives there."

Anna looks at Carla lost in thought, and although she doesn't move, her knot of hair slowly comes undone. "But when two people are **destined** for each other, surely they're bound to see each other again anyway? Whether they want to or not."

Carla turns off the projector with a sigh. "That's also a possibility, Anna."

Fortunately, Babsi butts in, "No way! It could take for ever. And besides: there are some people who never find the person they're destined to be with. You have **to make** some **effort**!"

I look at my friends. "OK, girls. Where do we begin?"

With the music schools. That was Carla's suggestion, of course. We set off to one because they're bound to have a list of all the trumpet teachers in town. Or maybe even HE is taking classes there.

A friendly woman is sitting at **reception**, hum-

---

to be destined for sth – für etw. bestimmt sein;
to make an effort – sich Mühe geben; reception – Empfang

ming to herself – I imagine because she's secretary of the music school. She gives us a list of trumpet teachers which is longer than we thought – much longer – and takes us into a large hall where an orchestra is in the middle of **rehearsing**. "If he plays with us, he'll be here," she **warbles**. "It's a shame you don't know his name."

Of course, it's a shame. Actually, it's almost tragic.

The strange thing is, we don't feel stupid at all. "Excuse me, we're looking for the cutest boy in town," I'd said.

Carla had quickly **qualified** this, adding, "That is, he's not bad looking!"

"Oh, come on, Carla, he's as sweet as sugar," butted in Anna.

Babsi blew a kiss with her mouth and sighed, "He's certainly got a great **bum**!"

How was the secretary meant to know who we were looking for with information like that? Not even the freckles helped, which I quickly added to his list of **distinguishing features**. But she certainly gave her best.

So now we're trying our luck in the big hall. The

---

to rehearse – proben; to warble – flöten;
to qualify sth – etw. einschränken/modifizieren;
bum – Po/Hintern;
distinguishing features – besondere Merkmale

orchestra consists of about forty people who are **tuning** their instruments. They don't even look up as we come in. There are only seven trumpeters – and HE is not one of them.

"I knew it: he's far too young for music school," I say as we leave.

"You never know, he could have been a **genius**," suggested Carla.

Then we have to drag Babsi out of the hall. She's fallen for the **timpanist** and is coming on strong with her Marilyn **seduction** routine. **Embarrassing**.

When we get back to my place, we call all the trumpet teachers **till we're blue in the face**. "Excuse me, do you happen to teach a really good-looking boy with freckles?"

They sometimes say yes, but when they describe him in more detail, it soon becomes clear that it can't be him. Red hair – no way! A bit **stocky** – certainly not! Glasses – not on your life! **Way off the mark**!

"OK. Then tomorrow we can take a look at the skateboarder scene," suggests Babsi and is thrilled

---

to tune – stimmen; genius – Genie; timpanist – Kesselpauker; seduction – Verführung; embarrassing – peinlich;
to do sth till one is blue in the face – etw. tun, bis man schwarz wird; stocky – untersetzt;
to be way off the mark – das Ziel um Längen verfehlen

because she thinks all the boys who skate are good-looking.

Carla taps her finger against her forehead. “You’re not going to throw yourself at one of those **halfwits** who’ve got nothing in their heads apart from riding a pavement with a block of wood on wheels, are you?!”

But Babsi is **oblivious to pain**. Except when it comes to Jorge.

We set off the next day straight after school. There’s a skater pipe in the square in front of the theatre, but before we start our investigation, we **treat ourselves** to a hotdog for lunch. All of us except Babsi.

“Have you any idea how many calories are in those lousy sausages?”

“If that’s the only thing that bothers you, then just drop it,” replies Carla with her mouth full. “A sausage like this is nothing more than simple matter transformed into **superfluous** energy.”

“Babsi’s just trying to spoil our appetite, right, Olli?” mumbles Anna, wiping her mouth respectably with a **cloth handkerchief**. Anna always

---

halfwit – Schwachomat; oblivious to pain – schmerzfrei;
to treat yourself to sth – sich etw. gönnen;
superfluous – überflüssig;
cloth handkerchief – Stofftaschentuch

has a cloth handkerchief with her. It's not her fault, it's because of her mother. I'm going to have to take the handkerchief she just used home with me, so that her mother doesn't notice that she's been eating ketchup. Otherwise Anna will go straight into **quarantine**.

Anyhow, **I can't be bothered** to deal with these problems. I just stare over to the half-pipe, trying to recognize somebody. One of the boys who he'd said hello to. Or maybe even HIM personally. I've brought the camera with me just in case. Maybe it will be easier to recognise me with it. And it's no problem that there's no film inside.

As ever the skaters are really childish. They whistle and laugh when they see us coming. Concentrated girl power. They're laughing because they're scared. That's boys for you. We **pretend** that we're interested in their tricks and sit down on the steps to watch. I've got the camera glued to my eye the whole time.

"HE isn't here," Anna whispers after a while.

Carla's face is full of **contempt**. She looks as if the mere sight of all these **boneheads** is causing her physical pain. I really don't know if Carla will ever

---

quarantine – Quarantäne;
I can't be bothered – ich habe keine Lust;
to pretend – so tun, als ob …;
contempt – Verachtung; bonehead – Dummkopf

fall in love. Just think what the guy would have to be like! “We’re in luck,” she says, jumping to her feet. “It looks like Prince Charming is no skater. Thank God!”

“What do you mean, ‘thank God’?” I say, feeling **cross**. “He hasn’t got any bad qualities until now.”

Carla just screws up her forehead.

Meanwhile Babsi starts talking to one of the skaters. “Can I try?” She smiles at him so broadly that he would probably do anything for her. *Would you drop your trousers please?* – He would do that, for example, guaranteed.

Anyhow, Babsi isn’t behaving so badly. She’s probably tried to **chat up** boys in the skater scene several times before in her life and is well practised. We go on watching as all the boys **flock around** her, helping her here, holding her there, or giving her tips. Babsi just beams the whole time, fluttering her eyelids and pouting her lips until she’s received enough admiration and we can finally go.

ABC have to go home. Yet another day without finding HIM! But no, I’m in no mood to give up right now. I get into the U3 at the photo shop and head towards the town centre. Maybe he’ll cross my path. Maybe I’ll **strike it lucky**.

---

cross – verärgert; to chat up – anbaggern;
to flock around sb – sich um jmdn. scharen;
to strike it lucky – einen Glückstreffer landen

I stay at the door of the train so that when we stop, I can look out at each platform to see if he gets in. That way I've got everything under control, and I just keep travelling with the tube **to and fro**. Of course, I can't buy a ticket each time, but I know what the **ticket inspectors** look like. It's always a sure thing: greenish-grey clothes, **old-biddy** shoes, acne scars from the past. I mean, who wants to be a ticket inspector, it's the **pits**!

As I travel back from the town centre for the eleventh time, I suddenly see HIM. As clear as day. There he is! He gets into the train two **carriages** down from me. Without thinking, I jump out of the train, but I only make it to the next carriage before the train sets off. I push and shove my way through the crowd to the last door so that I can easily change carriages at the next station, **craning my neck** to try and catch a glimpse of HIM! But I can't make him out in the crowd. At the next station I jump out again and run – right into a man wearing a greenish-grey uniform. "Tickets, please!"

Damn it, I've got more important things to do! "Excuse me, but right now is really bad." I try to

---

to and fro – hin und her;
ticket inspector – Fahrkartenkontrolleur;
old-biddy (ugs.) – altmodisch/Opa-;
to be the pits – das Letzte sein; carriage – Wagen;
to crane one's neck – den Hals recken

squeeze past him. All I can think of is my freckled Prince Charming who I just have to find.

But the man with the old-biddy shoes holds me back. "I can't help you there, young lady. First your ticket, then you can go."

I don't have one. He knows I don't. He shouldn't **make** such **a fuss** about it – a real bureaucratic carry-on – so that everybody turns around and stares at us. HIM, too. Or at least the guy I thought HE was. Because it's not him at all. I've been caught red-handed by some acne scarface all because of a complete stranger! Double damn it. After the ticket inspector has finally let me go, I'm **absolutely shattered** – and I have to walk all the way home.

Just as I collapse into a chair in the kitchen, utterly exhausted, I notice the strangely pleasant atmosphere in the place. A bit too pleasant for my taste. This must mean something. There are little vases all over the place with fresh little flowers and little bouquets. Classical music is playing somewhere, and Mum **is** completely **wrapped up in** arranging some tiny porcelain **elves** – yes, elves! – for her shop while humming to herself.

---

to make a fuss – Theater machen;
absolutely shattered – völlig erschöpft;
to be wrapped up in sth – mit etw. total beschäftigt sein; elf – Elfe

"Stressful day?" she asks with the most stress-free voice in the world.

"What's up?" I reply suspiciously.

Needless to say, all I get is a look of **blissful** ignorance. "What do you mean, what's up?"

I kick off my shoes without undoing the **shoelaces**. It's one of the few things that Mum can't stand, but this time she doesn't even register it. "I was caught **fare dodging** on the tube and I had to pay forty euros." I'll just **take** full **advantage** of the atmosphere if she's not going to tell me what's going on.

Mum stops humming. "What did you do that for?" she asks.

"There was nothing I could do about it. I … I was looking for someone and I kept having to … Oh, forget it. I can't explain." I wave my hand in tired **dismissal**. "Take it out of my pocket money over the year."

Mum turns back to the elves. She thinks for a second and says, "OK, I'll pay it for you."

Right! And now comes the **condition**. Four weeks of plucking thorns from roses? Sweeping the shop? Going with Mum to the **wholesale market**

---

blissful – glückselig; shoelace – Schnürsenkel;
to dodge the fare – schwarzfahren;
to take advantage of sth – etw. ausnutzen; dismissal – Abweisung;
condition – Bedingung; wholesale market – Großmarkt

at five o'clock in the morning and helping her carry things?

"We want to go out for dinner tomorrow evening. You know, meet the family. For the first time. You'll come, won't you?"

Who? What? I haven't got the **foggiest idea** what she's talking about. "Who is 'we'?" But as the words come out of my mouth, I know the answer already: the gorilla. Robert, Bob, Bobby! It's not over with him. **On the contrary**. I hadn't been paying any attention to the situation because I was too busy with my own stuff, and now we've got to the point of meeting the family.

MEETING THE FAMILY!

Mum looks up from her elves and smiles at me to the classical music. "You know who. What's that funny name you gave him?"

GORILLA!

---

to not have the foggiest idea – keine blasse Ahnung haben;
on the contrary – im Gegenteil

Meeting the Family

What else could I do but go? Even if Mum hadn't **blackmailed** me, I would still have ended up at the **laid-back** Italian restaurant where the two of them had decided we would meet the family. She would probably have **forced** me anyway. "You're coming with me, and that's that! No discussion!" she'd have said. Sometimes Mum is just another mother and not a friend. There are a few things which she thinks are important, and then she **calls the shots**, whether I like it or not.

She once **enrolled** me in a Russian literature reading circle. "I think it's important you get to know other things besides just hanging around with ABC." I went once. With twenty old people who took turns to read out of thick books which were written with the sole purpose of training your memory and were full of millions of impossible names, all of them ending in *-itz*.

ABC were horrified, of course. Meeting the fam-

---

to blackmail – erpressen; laid-back – locker;
to force sb – jmdn. zwingen; to call the shots – bestimmen;
to enroll – sich anmelden

ily, that's the taboo of the year, we were agreed about that. But what were we meant to do? Unfortunately, we are still **at the mercy of** the so-called adults.

"Look, I have to eat bio-sausages because they're meant to make you strong," Anna tried to **console** me. The comparison didn't quite hit the mark, although I would have liked to pack the gorilla into a bag full of disgusting bio-sausages and throw him into the bin.

That evening, again, Mum needed hours to do herself up. This time without my help. She didn't even ask me because she knew perfectly well what a bad mood I was in. Nor did she tell me to put something nice on myself. She wanted to spare herself the look of hate. So that's why I set off with her just as I was: in baggy jeans and the T-shirt with the hotdog stain on it from yesterday.

Adria is the name of the restaurant we go to, and there are pictures of Ferraris hanging all over the place, although they don't suit the atmosphere at all.

"Ciao, bella!" says the Italian restaurant owner to Mum when we come in and points us in the direction of a table reserved for us. A huge table. Far too big for three.

---

to be at the mercy of sb – jmdm. auf Gnade oder Ungnade ausgeliefert sein; to console – trösten

"Where do you want to …?" Mum asks me, and it's the first ever time she's shown an interest in where I want to sit.

"There, on the bench. Then I don't have to see him when he arrives."

Mum doesn't say anything to this. She just **wrinkles her brow** and sits down on the chair which the Italian restaurant owner has been waiting to push up behind her for ages.

A holder in the shape of a Ferrari **steering wheel** stores the salt, pepper, vinegar and oil. How marvellous! And how **appropriate** for a meeting-the-family dinner.

"Would you like something to drink?" the restaurant owner asks my mother.

She smiles at him nervously. "Thanks, we'll wait a bit."

She probably wants to choose her wine together with the gorilla. Then they can share a carafe and drink the same wine. If that's not a sign of love and **unity**! Mum knows what **befits** her.

"A glass of water, please!" I shout after the restaurant owner to put some distance between me and my mum. I hate water.

---

to wrinkle one's brow – die Stirn runzeln;
steering wheel – Lenkrad; appropriate – passend;
unity – Einigkeit/Zusammengehörigkeit;
sth befits sb – etw. schickt sich für jmdn.

Mum is all **twitchy** and keeps folding her serviette into animals, ships and hats. She keeps looking over to the door.

"Maybe he won't come?"

Mum glares at me with a look that says: come on, stop being such a **silly cow**. Make a bit of an effort. For my sake. It's the least I can ask for.

Not a chance! I'm not going to make it any easier for the gorilla to move in with us. I drum my fingers on the table so that Mum knows I'm not nervous, but I am bored.

All of a sudden her face breaks into a beaming smile, and she starts waving towards the door with her latest paper bird. "There he is!"

I don't turn around. He's coming over here anyway. The first thing I see is a double **pushchair** turning up on the scene, then the gorilla that's pushing it. There are two babies sitting in the pushchair. They look identical and have obviously decided they're going to sing "lalalalalalala" at a deafeningly, monotonous volume.

"This is Robert. You've met already," Mum begins the process of meeting the family. "And this is Fritz and Franz. Ha, ha, who's who again?"

So that's it! The gorilla has got kids **into the bar-**

---

twitchy – aufgeregt/zappelig; silly cow – blöde Zicke;
pushchair – Buggy/Kinderwagen;
into the bargain – darüber hinaus/noch dazu

gain. Little kids! Screaming, shrieking babies! The shock is almost unbearable, and my eyes go blurred. By the time they've regained their focus, the gorilla's giant **paw** is dangling in front of me. "Hi there, Olivia!" Sure, the guy says 'hi there'!

"Good evening!" I reply and give him the **wobbliest**, most limp, jelly-like handshake of all time.

Mum looks at me sternly. "Olivia, would you be so kind as to get two high chairs for the babies?"

Me? Why me? What have I got to do with the left and right hand of the devil, the two little beasts that are rocking wildly in their double pushchair, throwing their playthings across the restaurant? Really well brought up! Respect!

The Italian restaurant owner comes hurrying over with two high chairs. He's **over the moon about** the *grande famiglia* and doesn't seem to be at all bothered when the little **brats hurl** their baby's bottles at the Ferrari pictures. "Bambini! Che carino!"

"Pffffr!" Carla's sneering impression of a horse, performed live by me and met by a stern look of warning from my red-cheeked mother.

Once everybody has settled down and Mum and the gorilla have chosen a red wine together, things

---

paw – Pranke; wobbly – wabbelig;
to be over the moon about sth – über etw. überglücklich sein;
brat – Balg; to hurl sth – etw. schleudern

don't get any better. The left and right hand of the devil are sitting in their high chairs at the end of the table – far too close to me – and are **mutually** trying to **poke** each other's **eyes out** with the **cutlery**. Part of me would like to know what would happen if they actually succeeded, but unfortunately I – of all people – **bear the** sole **responsibility** for having to keep tearing the cutlery out of their hands. Then I have to get a cloth because one of the devils has spilt my water.

The gorilla orders spaghetti for the children. Just the right thing in my opinion. I only order another glass of water – I've suddenly lost my appetite – while Mum and the gorilla decide to share a starter.

"We can always see if we're still hungry after," **purrs** my mother and gets a kiss. No one knows why.

The gorilla gives his two little brats a piece of bread each, and this keeps them quiet for two whole seconds. He folds his hands and smiles at me. What?

I don't smile. You can wait **till the cows come home** for that, **ape**-man!

---

mutual – gegenseitig;
to poke sb's eyes out – jmdm. die Augen ausstechen;
cutlery – Besteck;
to bear the responsibility – die Verantwortung tragen;
to purr – schnurren;
till the cows come home – bis in alle Ewigkeit; ape – Affe

"Where's Number Three?" asks Mum, informing me that Robert has got another son.

Great news.

"I don't know where he's got to. He'll turn up. Paul's the same age as you, a bit older, but that's not a bad thing for a man and a woman, is it, Christie?"

No, I'm about to puke all over the table. What is the man thinking? That his stupid son will be of the least interest to me? And my mother is called Christina! But I have the **sneaking suspicion** that it won't be long before he starts calling her 'sweetie-pie', just because he can't think of any better **pet name**.

The restaurant owner comes with the spaghetti and puts it in front of the noses of the left and right hand of the devil. Mum starts cutting up the spaghetti for one of them.

"Can you do that for … Franz?" she asks me.

The gorilla smiles. "Fritz. But don't worry, it takes time to **get the hang of** it!"

What? Time? Mum and I don't have any time. I have no intention of taking any time to get the hang of Fritz and Franz, or anything that has the slightest thing to do with the gorilla.

I try to cut the little brat's spaghetti, but he keeps trying to grab my hands, shouting, "Olliolliolliolli-

---

sneaking suspicion – leiser Verdacht; pet name – Kosename; to get the hang of sth – auf den Trichter kommen olli!" and slapping me in the face with his greasy fingers.

"The best thing to do is to put him on your **lap** and feed him yourself," suggests the gorilla, and as far as he's concerned, it probably is the best thing to do. He hands the little brat over to me with a smile, and there's no way out of it.

"Olliolliolliolliolli!"

"Oh, here comes Paul!"

Now for the next disaster, I think as I hold the spoon of noodles up to the left hand of the devil's tightly closed mouth. "Eat it, for crying out loud!" I roar at the little brat, and all of a sudden, I find myself looking at the freckled Prince Charming who's standing at our table.

"'aul, 'aul!" screams the child on my lap, waving his arms about wildly. In doing so he knocks the spaghetti off the table and it **spills** all over me. Spaghetti with tomato sauce. Perfect.

I feel like my body has just turned to stone. Not because of the spaghetti, but because of Paul. So that's his name. And he's the son of Mum's beloved gorilla. How is it possible for a gorilla to produce such a good-looking son? I stare at HIM – HIM, this boy called Paul – and barely register that Robert takes the left hand of the devil out of my lap and Mum starts **scraping** the spaghetti off me.

---

lap – Schoß; to spill – verschütten; to scrape – kratzen

Paul grins at me, and I just think: that was lucky with the spaghetti – at least he won't notice the hotdog stain! Because right now I look as if someone has just dragged me out of a **cesspit**.

The restaurant owner serves the starter and a large portion of ice-cream with **sparklers** in it. "*Dalla casa* for all the *famiglia*!"

The little brats are given two spoons and then they **demolish** the ice-cream. Mum and the gorilla share the starter – she feeds him and he feeds her! And Paul, Paul sits down next to me. Paul, the boy from my Super 8 film. The boy I've spent days looking for. The trumpet player with the freckles. I don't know what to say, I can't think of anything, and I look on in fascination as he manages to feed the ice-cream into his two little brothers' mouths without making any mess, completely hassle-free.

He grins. "It takes time to get the hang of it!"

Yeah, time. That's something we have, Paul and I. What a **stroke of luck** that he's the son of gori… of Robert. How often does that mean I'm going to see him now? After all, we're all one *grande famiglia* now.

I smile back at him and just nod idiotically. I expect he thinks I can't speak. I **rack my brains**.

---

cesspit – Klärgrube; sparkler – Wunderkerze;
to demolish – vernichten; a stroke of luck – ein Glücksfall;
to rack one's brains – sich den Kopf zermartern

What can I say to him? I can nearly always think of something. "Where's your mum?" I ask in the end.

Paul's face immediately **clouds over**, and he stares at the bald head of his brother. "She ran off!"

Mum looks at me **reproachfully**, and I have to admit that she's right. That was a great topic of conversation you picked on!

"I'm sorry …" I mumble.

Then Paul looks at me – in a really nice way, unbelievable – and smiles a bit again. "It's OK. What's true is true!"

---

to cloud over – sich verfinstern; reproachful – vorwurfsvoll

ABC on the Street

"What's true is true! – How can anyone come up with a phrase like that? And a man at that!" Babsi is **staggered**.

ABC are walking along the street together, side by side. Babsi on the left, Carla on the right, Anna in the middle. They're on their way back from Olli, who's completely **beside herself**.

"Which still needs proving!" mumbles Carla.

"What?"

"That thing about being a man!"

Anna's cheeks are slightly reddened from all the excitement. "It so amazingly romantic, don't you think? Like in a movie." Anna makes a swinging gesture to illustrate the immensity of the romance, and Carla and Babsi have to take a step back.

"You're right. A young, innocent girl falls in love with her brother. That would make a great movie," says Babsi with a grin.

Anna stops in her tracks and looks at her **uncomprehendingly**. "But Paul isn't Olli's brother!"

---

staggered – fassungslos; to be beside oneself – aufgelöst sein; uncomprehending – verständnislos

Babsi finds the idea so wicked she can't stop grinning. "He is **to a certain extent**."

"Her **stepbrother**," points out Clara. "That happens in the best of families."

Anna is **incensed**. "But Olli's mum and the gorilla aren't even married. You two are crazy. You're just jealous. Didn't I say it all along: love knows no **boundaries**? True love always finds its way!"

"How do you know he loves her?" Babsi asks with a wink to Carla.

"That's obvious. He … he … you know, he smiled at her in a certain way. Weren't you listening?"

Carla gives Babsi a wink. "What kind of way, Anna?"

Anna stops in her tracks again, a highly concentrated expression on her face. Babsi and Carla look at each other expectantly, trying to hold back their **impending** laughter. Anna smiles the way she thinks he smiled, just as she imagines it.

Babsi pretends to **melt** in front of Anna and collapses on the pavement. "Do it again, Anna!"

Carla shakes her head and walks on.

Anna follows her, offended. "Is Babsi **taking the**

---

to a certain extent – in gewissem Maße;
stepbrother – Stiefbruder; incensed – empört;
boundary – Grenze; impending – drohend;
to melt – schmelzen

mickey out of me or something? Say something, Carla!"

"**Taking the piss**, Anna, it's called taking the piss!" Carla rolls her eyes.

Babsi catches them back up. "What's going to happen next?"

Carla wrinkles up her brow and cleans her glasses. "Either he'll try and **make a pass** at her, if he **fancies** her …"

"… and there can be no doubt about that!" butts in Anna.

"… or he won't do anything because he doesn't fancy her. It's as simple as that," Carla finishes off her theory, **unruffled**.

"Rubbish!" disagrees Babsi, and at the end of the day she's more of an expert in matters of love than Carla. Much more. "There are a million nuances in between. What if he's just shy and hasn't got the **guts** to make a pass at her? Or he's **level-headed** and thinks: I can't go out with my sister."

"But Olli isn't Paul's sister!" contradicts Anna.

Babsi puts her arm around Anna's shoulders from the left. "Not yet," she whispers.

---

to take the mickey out of sb – sich über jmdn. lustig machen;
to take the piss – verarschen;
to make a pass at sb – sich an jmdn. ranmachen;
to fancy sb – auf jmdn. stehen; unruffled – gelassen;
guts – Mumm; level-headed – vernünftig

Carla does the same from the right. "Stepsister," she corrects.

Anna **breaks out of their clutches** and stands right in front of her two friends. "So what? Is it illegal?"

"Not at all. It's not illegal!" says Babsi with a grin. "Everything's fine!"

Carla's face clouds over. "Let's just wait and see!"

---

to break out of sb's clutches – sich aus jmds. Klauen befreien

Skip Refuse and Paul

Sunday morning. That means breakfast with Mum. Today I'm going to get it ready. I don't think I've ever done this before, but I couldn't sleep anymore. So I might as well get breakfast ready instead of **tossing and turning** in bed and thinking of Paul. Paul!

I should have known that was his name. The name was made for HIM. He could only be called Paul.

I've already bought some fresh **rolls**, and I'm keeping them warm in the oven so that the room smells of them. No toast today. Real fresh rolls today. And, of course, little Tyrolean animals made of butter. Music. I need music. Mum likes **soppy** rock songs – she's got all the CDs – and although they usually turn my stomach, for some reason I'm in the mood for them today. I don't know why, but since Paul turned up at the *Adria*, I've been utterly at peace, like I was made of **cotton wool**.

Meeting the family was really harmonious in the

---

skip refuse – Sperrmüll;
to toss and turn – sich hin- und herwälzen; roll – Brötchen;
soppy – schmalzig; cotton wool – Watte

end. OK, so I didn't say anything. That was Paul's fault. But I had a permanent smile on my face, even when the left and right hand of the devil were allowed to run around the restaurant, pulling off one **tablecloth** after another. No one thought it was funny apart from the Italian restaurant owner. And me, I just grinned. It was enough just to be sitting next to Paul. There was nothing more I wanted and nothing more I'll ever need either.

"Mum! Breakfast!" I light two candles to soppy Sarah Connor music and take the rolls out of the oven.

"You have to wait for him to **make the first move**, if you know what I mean," Babsi had said. Of course, she knows all about **cunning** techniques with boys and she would never run after one. Never! She'd rather go without one. But Paul's not just anybody. Not for me anyway. For me he's something really special.

"There's nothing wrong with taking steps towards each other if you like each other," objected Anna.

"There's a whole lot wrong with it," claimed Carla. "If only the fact that this is about a guy. **Hands off**, that's my advice. It'll only be trouble.

---

tablecloth – Tischdecke;
to make the first move – den ersten Schritt tun;
cunning – raffiniert; hands off – Finger weg

But if you just can't leave it, Olli, if there's no other way, then it makes no difference who sets off along Bad Luck Road first – you or him."

I love girls, really, and I'm so happy that I have female friends who are so interested in me. It's good to hear their different opinions. But in this particularly special case, I'm just going to do what I want. And I want to see Paul as often as possible. And I'm talking about now. Today. **Without delay**.

At least he thought I was nice, I know that for sure. You can feel things like that. The number of times I caught him looking at me **out of the corner of his eye**! You notice things like that, even if you're not looking. Isn't that just fantastic? Especially arranged by the god of love: HE checks me out from the side, and I can tell he's doing it. I can raise my head a little so that I don't have a **double chin**, and subtly raise the corners of my mouth just a fraction. Just like Meg Ryan. She's an expert at that. She doesn't look as if she's actually smiling, just **on the brink of** smiling, anything but **grouchy**, always positive. And that's what you want to see out of the corner of your eye, isn't it?

---

without delay – unverzüglich;
out of the corner of one's eye – aus dem Augenwinkel;
double chin – Doppelkinn;
to be on the brink of sth – kurz vor etw. stehen;
grouchy – griesgrämig

Yes, how often did he actually look at me from the side, **inconspicuously** … or so he thought? The first time was as I was thinking about what to say. The second time was when the left hand of the devil pulled the tablecloth onto the floor, taking with it all the cutlery and dishes, and the Ferrari steering wheel with the salt and pepper. The third time was …

"Good morning!" says Mum as she **traipses** sleepily into the kitchen.

For hours after she's woken up you can see the **creases** of the pillow she's slept on in her face. Sometimes I can still make them out when I visit her in the shop at lunchtime. I don't know if the gor… er, Robert has already spotted this **phenomenon**.

"What's all this about?" she asks as she drops down into a chair, staring at the basket of fresh rolls.

"What do you mean, 'what's all this about'?" Just because I've bought some rolls. Really!

Mum wrinkles her brow but doesn't say anything. Why should she? She's got it good.

Now, where was I? Paul, of course. I slice a roll in half and melt a butter animal on it. Paul. He smiled at me when we said goodbye. He's so … so open. He doesn't hide anything in his face. When

---

inconspicuous – unauffällig; to traipse – tapsen;
crease – Falte; phenomenon – Phänomen

he smiles, he really smiles. Not to get something, or to look good. Just to smile.

"Olli?"

I'm thrown off my train of thoughts.

Mum bites into her roll and looks at me. "I asked you something."

Really? I didn't hear a thing. "What?"

"I asked if you thought it was nice yesterday evening."

I **dip** my knife into the raspberry jam. It's very **runny** because it's homemade, and you have to keep dipping in a lot before you've spread it on your roll properly. "Mmm!" Was it nice? Just nice? No, it was fantastic! Sensational! Give or take meeting the family. Actually, it was **mind-boggling** when I come to think of it. Paul and I got close to each other, **inevitably**, there's nothing anyone could do about it. Because we're a family that's been brought together. "I wouldn't have a problem if we met up more often," I suggest, **tilting** my roll to and fro to make the jam run.

"Yes, we could do that." I think my mum is now completely and utterly confused.

"Where do they live anyway?" I ask, because if I don't know that, then my whole plan won't work.

---

to dip – tunken; runny – dünnflüssig;
mind-boggling – irrsinnig genial;
inevitable – unausweichlich/zwangsläufig; to tilt – kippen

My plan is to casually turn up at Paul's place today. **Under the pretext of**: *I've got something for the little ones!*

"On the Bond Street **housing estate**. When you've got three children, it's better to have a little house, don't you think? It's only a **terraced house**, not really our style, but …" Mum just continues talking. Sure. She likes talking about Robert.

But I'm not listening to her anymore. I know all I need to know, and now there's absolutely nothing to keep me at this breakfast table. As I get up, my chair falls over. "I have to go," I mumble.

When Mum asks, "To the flea market?" I decide not to **enlighten** her. She tears my raspberry jam roll out of my hand, and I disappear into my room.

After all, I have a lot to do. Do myself up, for instance. What shall I wear? Now that I know I'm going to be meeting Paul, I can make myself a bit chic. Not like yesterday. And I have to get a present for the hands of the devil. Something from my **collection**. Maybe a **tin can**? I've got endless amounts of them in all shapes and sizes. Yes, they can have two large tin cans, the Turkish ones, the ones that

---

under the pretext of – unter dem Vorwand;
housing estate – Siedlung;
terraced house – Reihenhaus;
to enlighten sb – jmdn. aufklären; collection – Sammlung;
tin can – Blechdose

contained olive oil. As drums. I mean, that's just perfect for them.

The cans are in the storeroom. I climb up to the attic, where the dust is sparkling in the sunlight, and all of a sudden my heart starts to **pound**. The mere thought of Paul's brothers and their tin drums, that's what starts it off. And because my heart is pounding so much, and because the big tin cans are, of course, right at the bottom of my collection, the whole pile crashes over.

"Everything alright?" calls Mum from downstairs, and I shout "Yeah, yeah" back. Just don't get caught now! Olli in the middle of a thousand tin cans in the dusty sunlight with a **tingling** heart and a look of **elation** on her face. Not now. This is my very own personal look of elation.

I still need half an eternity until I decide on the long jeans skirt and the top with the **embroidered flowers**. Then I'm off. Bond Street. Terraced house. Paul!

On the way I pick up a few sticks so that the devil's hands will have something to bang their drums with.

In Bond Street people have left out their refuse for the **skip**. Normally, of course, I would completely lose myself in all the little treasures which

---

to pound – klopfen; to tingle – kribbeln; elation – Hochgefühl; embroidered flowers – Stickblumen; skip – Müllabfuhr

are piled up in the street, free for people to take with them. But not now. Now I have to go to Paul.

It's **beyond doubt** which is their house. It can only be the one with the double pushchair in front of it, surrounded by several toy cars, bicycles, tricycles, beach toys in all variations and shoes, large and small. A pair of tatty trainers clearly **belongs to** Paul. That means he's at home. That means I'll ring the doorbell, and the door will open, and Paul will be standing in front of me. I slowly move my **index finger** towards the doorbell. My heart is pounding, and it feels like the doorbell and my finger are magnets – only from the same pole. They just won't meet. In the end my finger just circles around the doorbell. It refuses to make contact.

But the door opens anyway, even without my having rung the doorbell. Paul is standing in front of me with his trumpet case under his arm. "Hey! I didn't hear the bell!"

I just stare at him because he's smiling in a way that just drives me crazy. But I manage to pull myself together – God knows how – and do a little **drum roll** on the two oil cans. "I've got a little present for your brothers!"

Paul grins – in a completely different way from his usual smile. He points his thumb over his shoul-

---

beyond doubt – eindeutig; to belong to sb – jmdm. gehören; index finger – Zeigefinger; drum roll – Trommelwirbel

der. “They’ll be over the moon. They haven’t stopped talking about you all day. How did you do it?”

Right then the devil’s hands come tearing out of the house, **charge** right towards me and almost knock me over. They start running circles around me crying, “Olliolliolliolliolliolliolli!”

They make such a **racket** it’s impossible to continue our conversation. And they haven’t even got their hands on the drums yet. Paul grins, slips into his trainers without undoing the shoelaces – my mum would **hit the roof** – waves his trumpet case at me and is about to leave. I instinctively grab his sleeve while the right hand of the devil tries to clamber up my leg. Paul looks at me. What do you want? says the look in his eyes.

Yes, what do I want? “We could go and … together … er … there’s skip refuse here. You can find really great things there. Do you want to … later …?”

Paul nods. “OK, I’ll be back in an hour.”

Oh God, he wants to!

I watch him go and ask myself where he’s going. Not to the music school, and not to any trumpet teacher in town. We’d already **researched** that.

---

to charge – stürmen; racket – Krach;
to hit the roof – an die Decke gehen;
to research – recherchieren

Maybe I'll ask him later, when he comes back. In an hour. One long hour! It's spent in the endless racket of the devil's hands, who wildly charge at their new drums. It's spent in the smelly **haze** of fat from the **chips** which the **childminder**, Tetta, is cooking in the kitchen. It's spent **wading** through the chaos like it was a piece of long, tough rubber.

Then, just as I'm pretending to be a horse, and the left and right hand of the devil are sitting on my back, beating their drums and shouting "Hoppalli-hoppallihoppallihop," Paul turns up all of a sudden.

He sweeps the two boys off my back, and they don't even **utter** a word of protest. Paul has really got them under control. "So, that's enough of that. Now Olli belongs to me!"

What a beautiful way to put it! I stand up and do my best to sort my hair out, but if you don't have a mirror, you can never tell. Anyhow, it was a good idea to put on the tight, long skirt in which I can **hardly** move. I follow Paul and **stumble** into his room. The devil's hands **accompany** us with a drum roll, shouting, "'aulandolli, 'aulandolli!"

Paul **slams the door in their faces** and nods to-

---

haze – Dunst; chips – Pommes; childminder – Tagesmutter; to wade – wabern; to utter – von sich geben; hardly – kaum; stumble – stolpern; to accompany – begleiten; to slam a door in someone's face – jmdm. die Tür vor der Nase zuschlagen

wards the window. "It's raining. I just have to find the umbrella."

I love him just for the fact that he didn't say, "*It's raining. Why don't we do the skip refuse some other time?*" But as I take a **furtive** glance around his room, I understand why. **He's** really **into** old things, like me. "Do you collect junk as well?"

Paul **appears** behind a pile of junk. He pulls out an umbrella. The umbrella from the dustbin. The one I wanted. Our love-umbrella, **brand new**. "You, too?" he asks. "I love repairing things, getting things back on their feet. Like this umbrella, for example." He opens it so that I can see that it's in perfect condition. "It was in such a bad state, **unusable**."

"I'd have made a photo stand out of it," I find myself saying. "If *I'd* have found a broken umbrella, that is."

Paul looks thoughtfully at the umbrella, and I can tell he can't really **picture** it. So I explain to him. "I like redesigning broken things into something completely different, something new! If that umbrella didn't have any covering, then you could open it up and clip your favourite photos onto the

---

furtive – verstohlen; to be into sth – an etw. interessiert sein;
to appear – erscheinen/auftauchen;
brand new – funkelnagelneu; unusable – unbrauchbar;
to picture sth – sich etw. vorstellen

arms with a clothes peg. Or hang up the cut-out sections of a Super 8 film. Just for example."

Paul smiles at me. "Not a bad idea!"

Then we set off. It's not really raining, but it is **drizzling** a little bit. It makes no difference to me when I'm **rummaging** through skip refuse. Apparently not to Paul either. The umbrella just hangs unopened from his arm.

We rummage through **peeling** shelves and **damp** old-biddy armchairs, **standard lamps** without a **lampshade** and computer monitors without any glass in the screen. I find an old accordion which only goes *pfffft*, and Paul finds a bike without any tyres. He's determined to give it a second chance. That explains why so many bikes are parked in front of his house!

All of a sudden, Paul spots two office chairs **on their last legs**. They don't have any stuffing, but the wheels are intact. "OK, let's have an office chair race!" he says and sets them up next to one another.

I know exactly what he means: we both sit down on a chair, the **backrest** to the front, leaning forwards against it, and then we use our feet to **pro-**

---

to drizzle – nieseln; to rummage – wühlen; to peel – abblättern; damp – feucht; standard lamp – Stehlampe;
lampshade – Lampenschirm;
on their last legs – fast unbrauchbar; backrest – [Rücken]lehne

pel us down the street – for which a tight, long skirt is not the ideal clothing! "First to the **advertising pillar**!" I shout and off we go.

We kick our legs like mad, and sometimes Paul is in the lead, sometimes me – depending on who's laughing more at the time. In the end, it's me who gets to the advertising pillar first, but then I **lose my balance** and crash into a pile of **cardboard boxes**. Paul ends up laughing so much, he loses control as well and crashes in behind me. Then we lie amongst the cardboard boxes for a bit and watch the rain drizzling down onto our faces.

"How can you **bear** being beaten by a girl?" I say, grinning at the sky.

"I can't. It's unbearable," Paul groans and giggles.

After that we rummage through the whole of Bond Street and the next street as well. By the time we've finished, it's really started to rain. Paul opens the umbrella and pulls me under it. Really close. There's no other way. It's a one-man umbrella, so there you go. With our arms full of **goodies**, we head back home, the rain splashing around us, but we remain dry. Because we're really close.

---

to propel – antreiben; advertising pillar – Litfaßsäule; to lose one's balance – das Gleichgewicht verlieren; cardboard box – Pappkarton; to bear sth – etw. ertragen; goody – tolle Sache

"What do you think of my dad and your mum being together?" Paul asks.

What am I meant to say to that? Right now I'm happy about it, but only because of Paul. "Well, you know, it's a bit strange when you've always done everything together, just the two of you."

Paul laughs and nods. "Do you know what I called your mum?"

No idea.

"**Daft bat**!"

I'm almost angry. My mum isn't a daft bat, not at all! "Your dad's called gorilla!" I say a bit too loud.

Paul stops in his tracks and takes my arm. "Hey, nothing against your mum. It's just not that easy **to come to terms with**."

I smile at him because my anger has already passed, and I give him a nod.

We continue walking, and Paul tells me that my mum's not called that anymore. "It's over."

"And why's that all of a sudden?"

Paul shrugs his shoulders. "No idea. Maybe because no one can be a daft bat when they have such a nice daughter."

---

daft bat – doofe Schrulle;
to come to terms with sth – sich mit etw. abfinden

A Kiss?

"Oh my God, I've got **goose pimples** all over!" Anna **can barely contain herself**. And rightly so! This is enough to **bowl** anyone **over**.

Anyone apart from Carla, of course. "It's easy to say something like that. Psychological **warfare**, it's called. Men say things like that and the average woman just melts. No matter what the guy does after that, there's no way the woman can be convinced he's a complete arse."

Babsi moves her head from side to side. "Well, no one has ever said anything as nice as that to me so soon. Not too pushy, but convincing and straight from the heart. He's interested in you, that's for sure."

"Boys are always after the same!" growls Carla.

But she won't succeed. No way. She can't **spoil** the way I've been feeling since I heard him say those words: pure happiness.

After we got back to Paul's, we drank a hot

---

goose pimples – Gänsehaut; to barely can contain oneself – sich kaum halten können; to bowl over – umhauen; warfare – Kriegsführung; to spoil – verderben

chocolate. The childminder, Tetta, had gone by then, and Robert had come back from work. "That was a really good idea of yours," he said to me with a grin and pulled a face as the left and the right hand of the devil came running into the kitchen, drumming loudly.

I shrugged my shoulders. "They're having fun anyway!"

Then we discussed the next evening. Robert wanted to go to the theatre with Mum, Paul had **re-hearsals** for a church concert at the same time – so that's where he goes! – and the childminder, Tetta, was only for day care, not evening or night care. That meant: no one was there for the devil's two hands.

"Then you'll just have to cancel your rehearsal," said Robert.

But Paul was of another opinion. "Or you don't go to the theatre. How about that?"

"I can do it!" I **blurted out**. First of all, I didn't want them to argue, and secondly – a considerably more important reason – I'd be able to spend an entire evening where Paul lives. And at some point he would come back from his rehearsal anyway.

Of course, they were both **thrilled**.

"It's really very easy," Robert told me, shouting

---

rehearsal – Probe; to blurt sth out – mit etw. herausplatzen; to be thrilled – sich sehr freuen over noise of the drums. "You won't even notice them. I'll put them to bed beforehand. You'll just be there for an emergency really."

"Which will never happen!" added Paul.

And now the time has come. I have to go in a minute. ABC are here. They wanted to hear exactly what happened, of course, but they're also here to make sure I get their very best advice.

"You just wait until Paul comes home, and then – wham – you go for it!" explains Babsi from the depths of my **wardrobe**. She's looking for the ideal combination of clothes for me.

Anna tries to **twirl** my hair up, pinning it up with about four thousand **hair clips**.

"I'm so excited!" I murmur.

"You don't have to go." Carla is lying on the floor, **leafing through** a women's magazine with contempt.

"And when he comes home, make sure you're lying on the sofa like this." Babsi throws herself onto my bed in an unbelievably sexy pose. Breasts **thrust forward**, her legs **chastely** at an angle, her

---

wardrobe – Kleiderschrank; to twirl – zwirbeln;
hair clip – Haarspange;
to leaf through sth – etw. durchblättern;
to thrust sth forward – etw. nach vorne schieben;
chaste – keusch

head **propped up** on her hand and her hair hanging casually over her shoulder. The very picture of Marilyn Monroe. "Hallo, Paul! Is that you?" she says in a husky voice.

Carla pulls her face. "What a load of rubbish. She can see it's him!"

Anna claps her hands and puts on her embarrassed expression. It's like this: she turns red and can't look anyone in the eyes. "Do you think you'll kiss?" she whispers.

"That'll be the least they get up to!" Babsi takes off her mega-sexy pointed **bra** and throws it over to me. "You should wear that. Just in case!"

"Rubbish!" I throw it back to her. "I'll look ridiculous. I could fit in there three times over." Unfortunately. I'm no competition for Babsi's **bust**.

"That's going too far!" cries Anna indignantly, and Carla **pipes up** from behind her magazine: "Why not? Then she can get it over and done with! Does anyone want to hear their horoscope, even if it's **made up** by some unemployed German Studies student?"

Anna and Babsi want to hear theirs, and I start putting on what Babsi has looked out for me.

I'm just hearing that the stars are **well-disposed**

---

to prop up – aufstützen; bra – BH; bust – Oberweite; to pipe up – sich zu Wort melden; to make sth up – etw. erfinden; to be well-disposed for sb – jmdm. gewogen sein

for me and I should definitely take steps in matters of love, when Mum comes in looking very stylish. "Excuse me ... can I go like this?"

So mother and daughter Pohlmann stand harmoniously beside each other, smiling awkwardly, getting the **last rites** from ABC. "Fantastic!" – "Divine!" – "It's OK!"

In the car Mum can barely contain herself. She keeps telling me how nice it is of me to be helping out with Fritz and Franz. "But do you know what I don't really understand?"

Of course, I know – why I'm suddenly being so nice about the whole thing.

"Why are you suddenly being so nice about the whole thing?"

Well, I can't tell you that.

When Mum and Robert leave, eye to eye, **immersed** in each other, everything really is fine. The left and right hand of the devil are asleep. I grab a malt beer from the fridge, settle down on the couch and turn on the television. Quiz shows. Quiz shows everywhere. I'm just proving to myself that I don't know anything, when the devil's hands suddenly appear in the doorway. Still really sleepy, but ready for action.

"Olliolliolliolliolli!" come their voices in stereo.

---

last rites – Letzte Ölung;
immersed – versunken

Aha, the emergency case which never happens.

First they're thirsty, then hungry, and in the end we play orchestra "like 'aul does". They play the drums and I play the saucepan **cymbals**. After that they say they're thirsty again, and in the end, I manage to get them back to bed, but only **on the condition that** I read them something. At some point in the middle of the fourth book I must have fallen asleep.

"Olli! Wake up!" Paul is standing over me, whispering to me with a grin on his face.

Great! Fantastic Marilyn-Monroe pose! I just hope I didn't **slobber** everywhere. The left and right hand of the devil are dozing quietly, and I creep out of the room behind Paul, trying at the same time to get my four-thousand-clip hairdo back into shape, without actually being able to see it. As Paul opens all the cupboards in the kitchen, I look at myself in the reflection of the microwave and find a complete **mess** on my head. Right, out with the hairclips.

"Man, I'm hungry! But there's never ever anything in this house. Never!"

"Nothing at all?" I pile up the hairclips on the kitchen table.

"Malt beer, a piece of dried toast and some

---

cymbal – Zimbel;
on the condition that … – unter der Bedingung, dass …;
to slobber – sabbern; mess – Durcheinander

mashed semolina powder, but no milk. Tetta goes shopping tomorrow."

Not even I can **rustle up** anything out of that. So I suggest getting a pizza in. The money which Robert left behind for me on the table should be enough.

Paul is chuffed and he orders two XXL pizzas with all the **toppings**. "Do you know that you've just saved a poor, very busy trumpeter from **starvation**?" He sits down next to me at the table and looks at me while I continue taking off the hair-clips. "Wait! You've missed one!" He takes the last clip out of my hair in a really natural way. He does it so gently that I don't even notice he's touching me. Except when a **tingle** goes through my body like an **electric shock**. Paul grins at me. "Now you look like you put your finger in a **wall socket**."

I grin back at him stupidly and only register what he's said seconds later. I hurry over to the bathroom and try to save what I can. As I look at myself in the mirror, I suddenly have the feeling that I'm not me anymore. All of a sudden my face is completely strange to me, and I touch it carefully, just to check that I can still feel it.

"Would you play me something on the trumpet?"

---

mashed semolina powder – Grieß; to rustle sth up – etw. schnell kochen; topping – Garnierung/Belag; starvation – Hungertod; tingle – Prickeln; electric shock – Stromschlag; wall socket – Steckdose

I ask Paul after I've just about managed to sort myself out and come back into the kitchen.

Paul **fumbles** with his trumpet case. He seems to be slightly embarrassed by the idea.

"Listen, if you can play in front of thousands of people in a church," I **gripe**, "then you can at least give your generous pizza-donator a **serenade**!"

Then he unpacks his trumpet and plays. Without saying anything. Without standing up or **making a fuss**. Just like that, on the chair. Just like the way he smiles, without anything behind it, just simple and honest. OK, it's only a short song, but still. When he's finished, we look at each other **bashfully** and neither of us knows what to say. Until a terrible racket tears us out of our silence. It's clearly coming from the kids' room.

"Oh no!" is all I can think, and the two of us run off to see if the devil's hands have woken up.

They have. We can tell by the fact that their beds are empty and the twins have disappeared.

"Shit," swears Paul.

Then we run through the whole house, shouting, "Fritz!" and "Franz!", looking everywhere, even in the cellar and the **broom cupboard**. But there's no trace of the brats.

---

to fumble – herumnesteln; to gripe – murren/schimpfen; serenade – Ständchen; to make a fuss – Theater machen; bashful – verlegen; broom cupboard – Abstellkammer

I start picturing all the possible scenarios, like they've drowned in the neighbours' **pond** or have been kidnapped. The phone will ring any minute. "*We've got the kids. You bring the money*," a husky voice will say. And we'll have to work out where we can get our hands on the millions. Why did they have to kidnap the devil's hands **of all people**, why the children of a poor social worker?

"Olli!" shouts Paul, and it sounds like he's **raising the alarm**. "The front door is open!"

Oh no. So they *have* been kidnapped! As if to **confirm** my worst fears, the telephone rings at that very moment.

"We haven't got any money!" I **shriek** into the receiver to make it perfectly clear to the gangsters.

But it's Robert. He wants to know if everything is going OK, and if the children are asleep.

"Everything's great!" I groan.

Robert tells me that there's money in the kitchen cupboard if we want to order a pizza.

I thank him and quickly hang up because outside Paul is calling for the devil's children. I don't think it's a good idea for Robert to hear him. I rush out to help Paul. "Have you found them?"

"No!"

---

pond – Gartenteich; of all people – ausgerechnet;
to raise the alarm – Alarm geben; to confirm – bestätigen;
to shriek – kreischen

The front door swings shut. Paul and I look at each other, then at the door. Needless to say, Paul hasn't got a key on him. But we spot the noses of the left and right hand of the devil pressing up against the glass of the door – them inside, us out.

"Fritz, Franz, open the door right now!" orders Paul.

I'm sure they'll do what he says. They always do what Paul says.

But **instead** they just shake their heads, shouting, "'aulandolli, 'aulandolli!" and disappear.

"Hey, you little bastards, open up right now!" Paul **rattles** the door like a madman. He's really angry, so I don't bother pointing out to him that he won't be able to open the door like that.

"Did you order some pizzas?" It's the man from the pizza service.

"Yes, but now we're outside, and the children are inside, with the money," I try to explain our problem to him.

He **grasps** the situation surprisingly quickly and puts away the pizzas. Then he points to an open window on the first floor and asks, "Have you got a **ladder**?"

Paul shakes his head and runs over to the tree. Its **branches** stretch over to the window. "I'll take the

---

instead – stattdessen; to rattle – rütteln;
to grasp sth – etw. begreifen; ladder – Leiter; branch – Ast

tree. – Just you wait. I'll show you little brats. You think you can fool around with me like that."

"Let me go, Paul. I'm an expert **climber**!" It's true. I can climb up anything. I have a special talent for it.

But the pizza man thinks this is a job for an adult, and he pushes us to one side and tries it himself. "If you don't mind, step aside for Giacomo – world champion in free climbing."

While he slowly **clambers** up the tree, Paul continues to try and **lure** the devil's hands to the front door. He promises them chocolate, kisses and hours of bedtime stories – and I have to **admit**, if I were the two brats, I would have opened the door ages ago. But they don't seem to be quite so hot on Paul's kisses. There's no sign of movement inside.

Giacomo reaches the height of the window. As he carefully tries to get to the window, going hand over hand along the branch, the police turn into Bond Street with their **siren** on.

"What is happening today?" says Paul. "Something's going on somewhere."

But Paul's wrong. The police are heading towards us because the neighbours thought that Giacomo was a **burglar**. The **custodians of the law**

---

climber – Kletterer; to clamber – kraxeln; to lure – locken;
to admit – zugeben; siren – (Polizei-)Sirene;
burglar – Einbrecher; custodian of the law – Gesetzeshüter

rush out of their car, shout at Giacomo to get down immediately, and tell him he's **under arrest**. They don't even let us **get a word in edgeways**. I feel like I'm in a bad film, or we're in some hidden camera gag. This can't be true! Giacomo, the free climber, starts clambering nervously down the tree. By the time he joins us, Paul and I have told the police what's really going on. So now he could climb back up. But he has no **intention** of doing so, which isn't a problem because one of the policemen says he can easily **pick the door lock**. At least that's what he says as he slips his **truncheon** back into his belt, playing Mr Big.

Giacomo decides not to hang around. He drives off on his Vespa and forgets to collect the money for the pizzas. But they're already cold anyway.

In any case, Mr Big doesn't manage to open the door, but his partner does, and we finally go into the house. We call out Fritz and Franz's name and run up the stairs. Instinctively. And we're right. The left and right hand of the devil are sitting in the **bathtub** in their pyjamas playing captains. The whole bathroom is underwater, and the two brats

---

under arrest – verhaftet/festgenommen;
to not get a word in edgeways – nicht zu Wort kommen;
intention – Absicht;
to pick a lock – ein Schloss aufbrechen;
truncheon – Schlagstock; bathtub – Badewanne

are having a great time playing with bottles of **shaving foam**, Robert's slippers and all the towels they could get their hands on in the water.

Paul freezes in the door, **dumbfounded**. It looks like he's **nailed** to the floor in complete shock. So I wade off towards the bathtub, turn the water off, lift out one **soaking wet** brat after the other and push them out of the bathroom. Needless to say, they scream like there's no tomorrow.

"Sorry," says Paul, clearing his throat and seeming to unfreeze. "Could you put them to bed? I think I would kill them right now."

I do just that, although the **murderous** thoughts are completely on my side. After all, those brats have ruined my evening with Paul. I just presume it wasn't intentional. I put them both into fresh pyjamas, dry their hair with a towel, and try to **kid around** with them a bit to keep them quiet. But it's not necessary. The devil's hands are dead tired. They fall asleep in an instant and look like two little angels. Kissable – if I weren't so angry with them.

In the meantime, Paul has **drained** the bathroom. He sits down on the edge of the bathtub and stares at me. I sit down next to him.

---

shaving foam – Rasierschaum; dumbfounded – entgeistert;
to nail – festnageln; soaking wet – patschnass;
murderous – mordlüstern; to kid around – Spaß machen;
to drain sth – etw. trockenlegen

"They're asleep!" I say, and he says, "Everything's dry!" exactly at the same time, and we just burst out laughing. We laugh so much that tears roll down our cheeks. We laugh so much that we have to **hug** each other. We're really close – our eyes, our mouths – like in a film: a short moment of **hesitation** before we forget everything and the **redeeming** kiss comes ...

But Paul **backs off** at the last moment and gets to his feet, shaking his head slightly. "Those two have always been a handful!"

Yeah, yeah. Hum. Oh, right.

Just then we hear someone opening the front door. At first we think that the left and right hand of the devil are running off again, but it's only Robert and Mum. They're so in love that they don't even ask how it went. They just look deep into each other's eyes the whole time. While they're busy doing that, Paul and I eat the cold pizzas and do our best to **avoid** eye contact with each other. Just don't dare to look.

Then Mum and I go home. We sit in the car in silence. Neither of us says a word. Mum is thinking about the kisses she got, and I'm thinking about mine. I mean, the ones I didn't get. Why did he back off? Why didn't he kiss me? What happened?

---

to hug – umarmen; hesitation – Zögern; redeeming – erlösend; to back off – zurückweichen; to avoid – vermeiden

The Second Chance

I don't know. I really have no idea. No idea at all. And ABC are equally at a loss. Why does someone suddenly back off like that? When everything is already a sure thing? When you already feel the warmth of the other person's lips! When you can almost already **sense** the feeling that is about to tingle through your body! Why does someone stop right then?

But now it's time for the **summer fête**, the biggest school event of the year.

"At least it will **take your mind off** things," said Anna.

We'll see about that.

ABC **are assigned to** the drinks counter in the school hall. That's one of the best jobs because you can see everything that's going on.

"And you have an **unobstructed** view of the boys!" according to Babsi.

---

to sense – spüren; summer fête – Sommerfest;
to take sb's mind off sth – jmdn. auf andere Gedanken bringen;
to assign sb to sth – jmdn. zu etw. einteilen;
unobstructed – ungehindert

Mmm.

The **school hall** is the place to party. Dark, loud music, dancing. And you can be sure there are no parents hanging out here.

"Forget the boys!" Carla advised.

Yeah, yeah.

Actually, I was meant to be helping out behind the **counter** as well, but then I thought of the Super 8 projector. "We could use it to put on a lightshow!"

Everybody thought this was a good idea, and that's why I'm now **head projectionist**. I went and rummaged through the storeroom for old Super 8 films. Because where there's a projector, there have to be films. It took ages because I kept thinking of me and Paul on the edge of the bathtub. I can feel it as if it were happening now, the way we almost kissed. And as I sat there in the dusty sunlight of the storeroom, feeling that feeling over and over again, I couldn't help shaking my head a thousand times. Why should someone stop right in the middle?

"I reckon the **premonition** of how it feels to kiss someone just completely bowled him over," contemplated Anna. "He wouldn't have **survived** the kiss itself."

---

school hall – Aula; counter – Theke;
head projectionist – Filmvorführchef;
premonition – Vorahnung; to survive – überleben

"Rubbish, then he wouldn't ever be able to kiss anyone!" Babsi was **filing her nails** and thinking. "For some reason or another he wanted it to be different."

But what reason could that be?

"He probably doesn't want to carry the consequences: relationships, responsibility, all that rubbish. Just a typical man: he'd rather spend his weekend hanging out in front of the computer with his **buddies** than have a great feeling. Without being disturbed by some **bird** who takes up his valuable male time!"

Babsi **hurls** the nail file at Carla. "You're crazy. He's probably just scared of his own **bad breath**!"

"Paul hasn't got bad breath!" I should know. After all, I was close enough to find out.

But now it's time for the summer fête. Eventually I find a whole **stack** of Super 8 films. I'll project them onto the wall while everybody dances to the flicker of ancient, fading pictures. It'll be great! And it's exactly the right job for me. I get to stand around in the dark and I don't have to **join in**. I really can't be bothered. I don't want to flirt with any second-rate boys. And I certainly don't want to dance. No, no. Just leave me in peace, the head pro-

---

to file one's nails – sich die Nägel feilen; buddy – Kumpel; bird (ugs.) – Mädchen; to hurl – schleudern; bad breath – Mundgeruch; stack – Stapel; to join in – mitmachen

jectionist in the dark who occasionally feels the I-almost-kissed-Paul feeling **surging up** in her. Melancholy all to myself.

I get dressed without even thinking about what to wear. I don't think because it makes no difference what the head projectionist in the dark is wearing. Then I rush to the door with my arms full of Super 8 equipment because ABC have rung the doorbell like hell four times.

"See you later at school," says Mum to me with a wave as I leave. Then she rushes over to answer the phone. "Olliiiii, it's for you!" she calls through the whole **stairwell** as I've almost reached the ground floor.

"I'm not heeeeere!" I call back up, and she shouts, "It's Pauuuuuul!"

I immediately drop everything, race up the stairs and tear the phone out of Mum's hand, completely out of breath. "Chwsh!" That's meant to be *hello*. *Hello* out of breath.

"Olli?"

I want to say *yes* and ask how he is and what he's doing and all that. "Chiii!" I'm completely **out of shape**.

"I just wanted to hear how you are and what you're doing and all that!" said Paul.

---

to surge up – aufsteigen; stairwell – Treppenhaus;
to be out of shape – keine Kondition haben

"Do you want to come to our summer fête?" I've finally got my breath back. But couldn't I have said something else? Something **non-committal**, indirect, diplomatic. But no, Olli blurts it straight out.

"Oh, is it your summer fête?"

"Yes. There's loads going on. Like in the school hall. A big party! How about it?" It makes no difference now anyway.

"OK!"

OK! Paul said OK. Paul is coming to the summer fête. Hello, where is **cloud nine**?

ABC ring the doorbell like crazy, and I really have to hurry now, particularly because I now have to put on something **decent** and give myself a splash of make-up. Oh God, my hair! All of a sudden, everything is different. I'm now not just the head projectionist in the dark, I'm also Olli who's going to be visited by Paul at the summer fête.

I don't know how long it takes, but by the time I finally make it **downstairs**, the girls are pretty angry. They're going to be late because of me, but when I tell them about Paul, they're really thrilled.

"This time you'll kiss, it's as clear as day. The guy **regrets** it." Babsi is wearing her blond Mari-

---

non-committal – unverfänglich;
cloud nine – Wolke sieben; decent – anständig;
downstairs – die Treppe hinunter; to regret – bedauern

lyn-Monroe **wig** and has painted her lips bright red. As ever she looks **stunning** and really sexy. "And I'm going to get a kiss today as well. I guarantee!"

"From Chorche maybe," giggles Anna, and that's just typical of her. She often drops a bomb just when you least expect it.

Babsi puts her arm around Anna's shoulders and **chuckles** back at her. "If you make any more of those **comments**, you'll have to go to the party dressed as you are!"

Anna is wearing a **flared skirt** and knee-length **stockings**. It's her mother's **fault**. That's why Babsi always brings some spare clothes with her on occasions like this, if only to make it less embarrassing for us.

Anna is immediately **taken aback**. "It was just a joke, Babsi. Honest. I bet they'll all want to kiss you, all of them!"

Babsi raises her eyebrows **in a huff** and turns down the corners of her mouth. Needless to say, she's just doing this to annoy Anna.

But as ever Anna doesn't even notice. "Even Lubo!" she says to **appease** Babsi.

---

wig – Perücke; stunning – blendend; to chuckle – kichern; comment – Bemerkung; flared skirt – Glockenrock; stocking – Strumpf; fault – Schuld; to be taken aback – erstaunt sein; to be in a huff – eingeschnappt sein; to appease – besänftigen

Carla rolls her eyes behind her glasses. Always the same hassle with men!

But now it's time for the summer fête, and Paul is coming. While Anna **gets changed** in a dark corner of the hall, I set up the projector. The music is good and really loud. Babsi and Carla start pouring drinks, and I put on the first film. It's shot on some **alpine pasture**, and it looks like my grandad when he was young. He's carrying a **walking stick** with lots of insignias on it. Everybody whistles and thinks it's a great effect. As the film rattles along, I lend ABC a hand and keep looking at the door. Paul said, "OK". But he didn't say when he would come. This is almost unbearable!

Carla **slates** the guys on the dance floor in a loud voice. They think they're cool, but the truth is they look like little sausages with gel in their hair.

Babsi thinks that one or two of the little sausages look quite nice, but in turn she slates the girls on the dance floor as they **wriggle around** in front of the little sausages feeling incredibly sexy. "They've got nothing **up front**!"

I really should point out to Babsi that it's unfair to say things like that because there's nothing anyone can do about it. But just then Lubo comes into

---

to get changed – sich umziehen; alpine pasture – Alm; walking stick – Spazierstock; to slate sb – jmdn. zusammenstauchen; to wriggle around – herumzappeln; up front – in der Bluse

the hall with his **entourage**, and his entrances always leave a big impression. His long thick hair is tied back in a **ponytail**, and one of his trouser legs is rolled up – probably to demonstrate for some **minority** group, but I haven't got a clue which one. He strolls through the hall, surrounded as ever by a handful of boys and girls, who, for some reason, are utterly **devoted** to him. He does a little boogie to the music and takes a look around.

"It's a **miracle** they don't follow him on their hands and knees and **fan** him with palm leaves," groans Carla. Needless to say, she doesn't like Lubo.

But if you're honest – and Anna, Babsi and I are honest – then you can only regard him with **admiration**. As long as you're not in love with Paul, of course.

Lubo stops in front of a patch of white flickering light on the wall. It takes me a second to register that the grandad film is over, and I urgently need to fulfil my duties as head projectionist. I rummage through the bag of films and take out a Bugs Bunny film. Perfect, old cartoons will look really good to our music. By now I'm pretty much a professional in threading the Super 8 film into the projector, and I don't even look up when it starts.

---

entourage – Gefolgschaft; ponytail – Pferdeschwanz; minority – Minderheit; devoted – ergeben; miracle – Wunder; to fan sb – jmdn. zufächeln; admiration – Bewunderung

All of a sudden, everybody bursts into laughter and shrieks. Old cartoons can't be that funny, I think, and I look up to see a scene from a hardcore porno being projected on the wall. Oh God, get that off quickly! How do I turn the thing off? All of a sudden I can't remember which **button** it is. And what's a film like that doing in a Bugs Bunny box? And why does Mum have something like that in the first place? The laughter around me gets louder and louder, mainly because, instead of turning off the projector, I've pressed the rewind button and the whole scene is now running **backwards**. Lucky Paul's not arrived yet! Where's he got to? I'm **in a** complete **muddle**. I just want to bring this embarrassing situation to an end. So I **tear out** the film. It **gets** all **tangled up**, and suddenly smoke starts coming out of the projector.

Then someone presses the *off* button, and the spectacle comes to an end. "I guess someone was trying to hide it in another box. My parents always did that!"

The person who's saved me is Lubo. Of all people. He's standing really close to me, threading the film out of the projector. He holds a burnt piece under my nose. "Anyhow, the fun's over now!"

---

button – Knopf; backwards – rückwärts;
to be in a muddle – durcheinander sein; to tear out – ausreißen;
to get tangled up – sich verheddern

Everybody settles down again and resumes dancing.

Lubo gives me the tangled pile of film and checks to see if the projector is still working. "What's your name?"

I **glance** over to the drinks counter and see ABC staring at me, Anna with wide-open eyes, Babsi waving her thumbs-up at me **frantically** – which can be roughly interpreted as meaning: *go for it!* – and Carla with her raised eyebrows.

I can't believe it. For months there was nothing I dreamed of more than of Lubo even **deigning** to glance at me. And now that I'm dreaming of other things – and above all of someone else – he's standing right next to me, asking me my name. Lubo! Me!

"Olivia," I just about manage to say. Then I look for a new film because the projector still works. **Just to be on the safe side,** I take one that is carefully labelled on both the **spool** and the box. Of course, it's still no absolute guarantee, but it's safer.

Lubo threads in the film. He does it like a real professional.

Babsi brings us two drinks with straws. She just couldn't stay behind the counter any longer. "Hello

---

to glance – blicken; frantically – wie wild;
to deign – sich herablassen; just to be on the safe side – vorsichtshalber; spool – Filmrolle

there, sweeties?" she whispers, but Lubo doesn't even look at her. So she leaves the drinks with us, whispers, "How *do* you do it?" into my ear and walks off.

"My **mates** and I always meet up on Fridays after school. At the boathouse on the lake. No big deal, you know, just hanging around a bit, going swimming and stuff. If you fancy it?" says Lubo, really casually.

I stare at the wall on the other side of the hall and don't even register that luckily enough I've chosen a really harmless film this time. My grandad as a young man is holding a small garden party in which someone is playing the accordion, although you can't hear it.

Is this true? Did Lubo just invite me into his **illustrious** circle? Am I meant to become a member of his **posse**? A few weeks ago I would have collapsed into his arms out of **sheer** happiness. Now it sounds like Lubo is talking to me from far, far away because everything is different since I met Paul.

"Olivia?" Lubo looks deep into my eyes and holds out his glass to me. "Cheers!"

He wants us to **drink a toast**. Lubo and me. I can tell that the entire female contingent of this hall

---

mate – Kumpel; illustrious – ruhmreich; posse – Gruppe; sheer – bloß/pur; to drink a toast – anstoßen

right now is **turning green with envy**, biting their pointed nails and asking themselves, "What's she got that I haven't?" I really have no answer to that, none at all.

All of a sudden, I spot Paul standing in the door, his hands buried in his pockets, looking around **insecurely**. I just leave Lubo standing with his glass raised. There's nothing else I can do. "Would you mind looking after the projector for a second?" I mumble and head off towards Paul, which is why the entire female contingent of the hall **breathes a sigh of relief** and Lubo looks a bit dumbfounded. But I don't care. I'm going to Paul.

He smiles at me. He's pleased to see me. Lubo is nothing **in comparison** to this. "Hello, Olli. It's not bad here!"

"Hi! Do you want a drink?"

Paul nods and I see the **craving** faces of ABC behind the drinks counter. At last they're about to meet Paul. Anna is bound to say something about Lubo, while Babsi will probably tell Paul about the porno, and Carla will **exude** a cold **aloofness** just to be on the safe side.

"But let's go outside," I suggest, and Paul agrees.

---

to turn green with envy – vor Neid erblassen;
insecure – unsicher; to breathe a sigh of relief – erleichtert aufatmen; in comparison – im Vergleich; craving – lechzend; to exude – ausstrahlen; aloofness – Zurückhaltung

We **stroll** through the school. There's something going on everywhere. We don't really know what to talk about, but it's still nice walking along side by side.

"Do you want to try knocking over some tin cans?" I ask Paul as we pass the **stalls** of the **lower years**. "But you'll lose again," I claim. "I'm **unbeatable**!"

Paul grins at me and pulls me over to the stall of cans – he touches me!

I'm not bad. I manage to knock all the cans over except for two. Two cans too many though. Paul has hammered all his down.

He puts his hands in his pockets and beams at me. "Sorry about that. I seem to be even more unbeatable at knocking down piles of cans!"

"Screwdriver or rose?" asks the Year 5 student, winking at me cheekily because, of course, he thinks that we're going out together, and so Paul will choose the rose.

Sure, it's Paul's big chance. I mean, he can say it to me now, like, through the flower. I can already tell that I'll **turn bright red**. Guaranteed.

"The screwdriver!"

I'm so disappointed that my heart drops into my

---

to stroll – schlendern; stall – [Verkaufs]stand;
lower years – untere Jahrgänge; unbeatable – unschlagbar;
to turn bright red – knallrot werden

boots. And my jaw, too. He chose the screwdriver! I've been **kidding myself** all along. There's nothing between me and Paul. At least, he feels nothing for me. That's why he didn't kiss me. It's **obvious**.

Paul smiles at me and ceremoniously gives me the tiny screwdriver. "I thought you'd rather have something you can use for your **handiwork**, is that OK?"

He noticed! He listened to me! He's interested in me! Paul is just more of a practical guy. I don't need the romantic type. Not at all. I was never into stuff like that. Thrilled to bits, I put away the screwdriver. It feels like it's **scorching hot**, at least to me it does.

I wander through my school at Paul's side, close to him, out of this world. All of a sudden, I see Mum and Robert and the two brats having a **sack race**. Paul freezes. He's spotted them, too. We look at each other. Neither of us wants to see our *grande famiglia*, so we make to escape.

Suddenly we hear the devil's hands shouting, "'aulandolli, 'aulandolli!" behind us.

"Shit, they've spotted us!" groans Paul. He grabs my hand and pulls me around the corner into

---

to kid oneself – sich etw. vormachen;
obvious – offensichtlich; handiwork – Bastelarbeit;
scorching hot – glühend heiß;
sack race – Sackhüpfen

a room. Once inside, he slams the door shut. "Ssshhh!" he hisses.

I'm standing really close up to Paul, **squeezed** together in the dark room. I've no idea where we are. I guess this is heaven. It's that beautiful.

We hear the left and right hand of the devil chanting, "'aulandolli, 'aulandolli!" outside, but they seem to pass us by.

Just after that we hear Mum and Robert calling, "Fritz! Franz!" as they desperately run after them. And they run right past us. We made it!

I smile at Paul and am just about to say something like "Saved!" or "Close shave!"

But Paul kisses me, and I'm in no position to say anything. My entire body tingles, and I don't ever, ever want it to stop. I lean into Paul, and he leans back onto something **flimsy**. It **gives way,** and Paul loses his balance. Me, too. We go crashing to the floor together.

Then our kiss is over because someone opens the door and turns on the light. We're in the biology storeroom.

"'aulandolli, 'aulandolli!" The devil's hands charge towards us. And towards Toni, the dusty, almost hairless school gorilla who couldn't take the weight of our kiss.

---

to squeeze – drücken/pressen; flimsy – leicht;
to give way – nachgeben

ABC on the Toilet

"They did it! They really did it! I knew they'd do it!" Anna is the third to come into the school toilet.

Babsi and Carla are already there. Olli is missing.

"Oh, come on, don't give me that. They only kissed, that's all!" Carla rolls her eyes.

She's sitting in the cubicle on the right, Babsi on the left, and Anna sits down in the middle one.

"Did I tell you or didn't I, Babsi? Come on, admit it!"

"We all knew perfectly well that he was going to kiss her, Anna. I mean, how often do you get a second chance in life? He'd be pretty stupid to **miss** it. And to have done it on top of Toni, our hairless friend!" Babsi sighs. "Unbelievable!"

"Do you think it was … you know … I mean … er … a real …?"

"With the **tongue**?" Babsi gets to the point.

"**Yuk**!" sighs Carla.

"No idea. She'll tell us in a moment. But I guess so, otherwise it wouldn't be a real kiss."

---

to miss – verpassen; tongue – Zunge;
yuk! – igitt!

"Did Schrödinger just **let you off**, Anna?" asks Carla. "I can't believe he **fell for** the toilet routine again!"

"He'd rather not have done it, **not on your life**! But what else could he do?"

"Have you already kissed with your tongue?" Babsi is still on the subject of what happened around hairless Toni.

"Never. I'm saving that up for Mr Right," says Anna with a **yearning** sigh.

Babsi is absolutely **horrified**. "Anna, you must be off your rocker. That could take **centuries**."

"How do you know? Maybe he's already got one foot in our garden. There's no reason why it should take so long. And if it does … then I can wait."

Silence. **No comment**.

"What about you, Carla?"

"I can do more than wait: I can just **do without** it, completely!"

Babsi leans against the toilet seat Marilyn style. "You don't know what you're missing!" she sighs. "But why does everybody fancy Olli all of a sudden? Even **holy** Lubo!"

---

to let sb off – jmdn. ziehen lassen; to fall for sth – auf etw. hereinfallen; not on your life! – beileibe nicht!; yearning – sehnsüchtig; horrified – entsetzt; century – Jahrhundert; no comment – kein Kommentar; to do without sth – auf etw. verzichten; holy – heilig

"People in love have something really special about them." Says Anna, probably with tears in her eyes.

"This whole love **rigmarole impedes** your senses and makes you a **slave**. People can think of nothing else, as anyone can see with the two of you. And Olli. She's talked about nothing but Paul for days. Paul, Paul, Paul. All of a sudden, she doesn't even care about things like the fact that her mum's in love. What's so good about that? Flat and **mundane**. That's all there is to it." Carla-lecture over.

"But it's the most important thing in life!" protests Anna.

"You can't be serious. What a horrifying thought! Being brain-dead as life's goal!" Carla is **in full swing**.

"Olli is happy!" objects Anna. "And that's not exactly what you sound."

"Wait and see," growls Carla **gloomily**. "The bigger they come, the harder they fall!"

"Where's Olli got to anyway?" asks Babsi, and no sooner has she said it than the three girls in the cubicles hear the door open.

Someone comes into the toilets. The girls immediately rush out of their **hiding places**.

---

rigmarole – Prozedur; to impede – behindern; slave – Sklave; mundane – profan; to be in full swing – voll in Fahrt sein; gloomy – düster; hiding place – Versteck

"Olli! At last! So tell us, did you kiss him with or without your tongue?" – "How long did you kiss for?" – "How many times?" Babsi and Anna bombard Olli with all their questions at once. But after a second they realise it's not Olli at all. It's not Schrödinger either, but – no – much worse …

"Chorche?" Babsi is horrified. "What are you doing in the girls' toilets?"

Jorge goes to his knees, grinning. "I'm looking for you, *tesoro*, only for you!"

Anna quickly **exits**, leaving Babsi and Jorge alone, but Babsi rushes after her. "You must be crazy! Leaving me alone with that **nutcase**!"

---

to exit – hinausgehen; nutcase – Spinner

The Hard Fall

"This time we had no other choice. We just had to kiss. It was magnetic. Pure **attraction**. Even if a magic **fairy** had come into the biology storeroom just beforehand and warned me that if I kissed him, I would die on the spot, I would still have kissed him. Just to **experience** it once. And he actually did it this time. He didn't suddenly break off in the middle. I knew it. You can always tell when someone likes you!" I try to explain to the girls why I'm so happy. How happy I am. **Infinitely** happy.

"Do you … I mean … er … did you kiss with … you know … Babsi, Carla, come on, ask!"

Babsi and Carla shrug their shoulders cluelessly. Sure, we all know what Anna wants to know, but she has no idea that we've guessed, and we're not going to say anything unless she has the guts to speak those words: **FRENCH KISS**!

Anna puts on her **conspiratorial** face and puts her arm around my shoulder. Her conspiratorial

---

attraction – Anziehungskraft; fairy – Fee;
to experience – erleben; infinite – unendlich;
French kiss – Zungenkuss; conspiratorial – verschwörerisch

face looks something like this: she narrows her eyes, raises her eyebrows and puts on a knowing smile. “Come on, tell me, Olli.”

“What do you mean, Anna?”

Carla and Babsi grin.

But I manage to keep a **straight face**. If you’re in love and things are working out, and if you’ve just kissed Paul, then you can do anything. Even keep a straight face. Even if you really want **to laugh your head off**.

“Then maybe you could organise a bit of contact between me and Lubo …?” suggests Babsi.

I wave my hand dismissively. Lubo? Who’s Lubo?

“Anyhow, it’s Paul’s turn to call you this time, Olli!” Babsi wants to make sure I don’t lose my **dignity** again.

I don’t think about things like that. For me it’s obvious: Paul will call any second. I know the kiss **got** right **under his skin**, just like it did with me. I can tell. I just know he’s thinking about me all the time, just like I am about him. No doubt about it.

The phone rings. There you go.

All four of us rush over.

“Olivia Pohlmann.”

---

a straight face – ein ernstes Gesicht;
to laugh your head off – sich totlachen; dignity – Würde;
to get under sb’s skin – jmdm. unter die Haut gehen

"Hello, Mrs Pohlmann. I hope I'm not disturbing you. I'm calling from the **opinion poll** institute *Bruder and Jacob*. We're currently doing a **survey** of women in their mid-40s. Do you still menstruate?"

I hang up.

And so it goes on. For days. For a whole week. For ever. I go through the three typical waiting phases together with ABC:

1. Euphoric phase

The only thing I talk about is Paul. The only thing I think about is Paul. I am Paul. The idea that anything could go wrong is **unthinkable**.

There is no shadow of doubt. Not even Carla can cause any. "It's about time he called! I mean, your magnificent kiss was two days ago!"

I don't even listen to her. Paul, I think, Paul, and Paul again.

2. Suppression phase

I kid myself that **I'm not bothered** by the fact that Paul hasn't called me yet. Even though I know perfectly well that the days are flying by, and it

---

opinion poll – Umfrage; survey – Erhebung/Studie;
unthinkable – undenkbar;
there is no shadow of doubt – es besteht nicht der leiseste Zweifel; suppression – Verdrängung;
I'm not bothered – es stört mich nicht

must be impossible for him to survive so long with out me. I pretend I'm really happy that he hasn't called because we wanted to shoot this Super 8 film anyway, and it means we've got a lot more time. – Unfortunately, we can't decide on what kind of film to make, and I **blow** the whole of the next expensive roll of film on recording our discussion.

I imagine all sorts of reasons why Paul hasn't called:

- he's broken his finger.
- he's at the **school country hostel** in Kirgizstan, and there's no telephone there.
- the kidnappers, who had originally planned to kidnap the left and right hand of the devil, **changed their mind** and chose to take Paul instead – a wise decision. He can't call, but every now and again he can send photos of himself holding the daily newspaper to Robert.

Paul doesn't call, and I decide to ask Robert. He's always calling and seems to be constantly here. He knows what to do in his situation.

"What's Paul doing these days?" I ask discreetly, praying that he gives me an answer that will make me happy. "*Paul thinks of nothing but you the whole*

---

to blow – verballern; school country hostel – Landschulheim; to change one's mind – es sich anders überlegen *day long. He's just scared of calling because he's worried you'll* ***turn him down****.*"

"Oh, you know, he's hanging around at home, playing the trumpet, **refusing** to help out with the housework – nothing special," says Robert, making me unhappy.

3. Weak phase – up to ***self-abandonment***

If that's the case, then was it all just a **lie**? Paul doesn't love me?

I begin to doubt. I fight with myself. I refuse to believe it, and I don't want Carla to be right. I don't want to hear Babsi telling me that other mothers also have good-looking sons, like Lubo for instance. And I can't stand it when Anna tries to show me **sympathy** and says it just means he wasn't my Prince Charming then, and reckons I gave my you-know-what – she means my tongue! – to the wrong person.

Maybe he really is just shy! Maybe everything's going wrong at the moment because he's just too scared to call and I'm playing hard to get, which is something I don't usually do. Really. Will I **lose face** if I call him? The worst thing would be if he turned me down, but even that would be better

---

to turn sb down – jmdn. abblitzen lassen; to refuse – verweigern; self-abandonment – Selbstaufgabe; lie – Lüge; sympathy – Mitleid; to lose face – das Gesicht verlieren

than this constant waiting. So I'll call him. Or should I ask the girls? They'd advise me against it, I know that. No, I won't ask them. I'll just call.

"Hello?"

I **hang up**. That was Paul, as clear as day. Which means he's at home and can answer the phone. Which means he could call me. But he doesn't. Why should I run after him, the arsehole? **Automatic redial**.

"Hello? Who's there?" he asks.

"Hello, it's me!"

Silence.

"Olli?"

"Yes!"

Silence.

"I just wanted to hear how you are."

"Fine."

Aha. He's fine. Well, then everything's just wonderful. So, now I can hang up. "Are we going to see each other again?" How can I **degrade** myself like this? How could I let that **slip out**?

Silence on the other end of the line.

"No, just kidding!" It's getting worse and worse.

"It's a really bad time for me at the moment. I'm stressed out because of the concert, you know."

---

to hang up – auflegen; automatic redial – Wahlwiederholung;
to degrade oneself – sich erniedrigen;
to slip out – herausrutschen

Oh, right. Of course, stressed out. That's why he couldn't call. "OK, no problem, then I won't disturb you any longer!"

Silence.

"See you around, Paul!"

Silence.

"Bye!" I'm just about to hang up. No one's left me hanging like this before.

"Olli?" I **jerk** the **receiver** back up to my ear. Thank God I heard him! "Yes?"

Silence.

"I'll … er … see you around!" Paul hangs up.

I stare at the receiver in horror: it's peeping like the line is **engaged**.

Paul hardly said a thing. It was awful. **Dire**. But at the end, he **changed his tune**.

Peep-peep-peep!

He didn't want me to hang up. He's thinking about me, but he's stressed out. Maybe he's just thinking: I'll call her when I've got time. We can't meet up right now anyway, and that would **hurt** her feelings.

Peep-peep-peep!

Rubbish. Don't kid yourself, Olli. Be realistic. But does he now know that I'm thinking about him

---

to jerk sth – etw. mit einem Ruck ziehen; receiver – Hörer; engaged – besetzt; dire – ätzend; to change one's tune – einen anderen Ton anschlagen; to hurt – verletzen

at least? Or does he think that I'll never **forgive** him? Perhaps he was in the middle of practising? His piece for the concert. That's why he was so unfocused.

Peep-peep-peep!

I hang up. **Nonsense**. The whole thing.

"I'll … er … see you around!" is what he said. That means he wants to see me, nothing more, nothing less.

I can't be bothered anymore, **churning** everything **over**, every sentence, every word. I don't want to keep thinking about what's wrong and what's right. Finished. Over. Paul is stressed out, and the woman who loves him is now going to pack him an anti-stress parcel. I go and get a prehistoric **basket** from the storeroom, pad out the inside with **chequered napkins**, thickly butter a few pieces of bread and mix a **redcurrant spritzer** in an empty bottle to give him energy. Then I record a cassette of smoochy songs. I don't put it in the basket yet, because I'm not sure if Paul likes things like that. Instead, I put in the **wind chimes** which I made from some metal leftovers. And just before I finish, I put in a cactus which I grew myself. All for Paul.

---

to forgive sb – jmdm. verzeihen; nonsense – Blödsinn;
to churn over – hin und her wälzen; basket – Korb;
chequered napkin – eine karierte Serviette; redcurrant spritzer – Johannisbeerschorle; wind chimes – Windspiel

I'm expecting ABC to turn up here any second, but I won't be here. There's nothing I can do about it. I'll explain to them later. After cheering Paul up.

I run along Bond Street like **Little Red Riding Hood** with my basket slung over my arm. My Bond Street, where I beat Paul in the office chair race. I don't care if the Big Bad Wolf suddenly **bursts out** of the woods on the left. I won't even see him. I can only see Paul's house as I head towards it. No one can **deter** me from my path. I see his trainers in front of the door. I ring the doorbell without thinking. Just don't think. Any second now Paul will open the door.

"*I've come all the way through the forest to bring you this anti-stress basket!*" I'll say. No, of course, I won't. Hello, Olli, concentrate!

The door opens and I find myself looking at a girl. She's about the same age as me, but she's blonde and taller. We **eye** each other **up** from head to toe without saying a word. Blonde, huge **boobs**, piercings, long thin legs, painted toenails. She raises her eyebrows. It suddenly shoots through my head that next to Paul's trainers is a pair of silly-cow boots. I saw them as I arrived, but I just didn't register them. Damn it, she's good-looking!

Little Red Riding Hood – Rotkäppchen;
to burst out – herausstürzen; to deter – abbringen;
to eye up – mustern; boobs (ugs.) – Brüste

"Yeees?" Miss Pretty asks, wrinkling her brow.

What am I meant to do now? Who is this? The new childminder? Tetta 2? "Is Paul home?"

Miss Pretty raises her eyebrows even higher and runs a hand through her blonde **mane** of hair. She just looks at me. Then she turns around and shouts into the **depths** of the house, "Paul!"

We wait. She doesn't let me in. I'm not allowed to **set foot** in the house where I very nearly kissed Paul. I can't think of anything to say, and Miss Pretty just eyes me up in silence.

Fortunately, the devil's hands suddenly come charging around the corner. "Olliolliolliolli!" They try to clamber up my legs.

I **bend down** to them and sink to my knees. It's the first time I've ever been happy to see them. "Hey, you little devils, how are you?"

Miss Pretty folds her arms over her huge bust and looks at us as **suspiciously** as she can while the left and right hand of the devil **take apart** the anti-stress basket.

"Hey, leave it alone! Hands off! That's for …"

Paul appears behind Miss Pretty.

"'aulandolli, 'aulandolli, 'aulandolli!" shout the devil's hands, and Miss Pretty puts her arm around

---

mane – Mähne; depth – Tiefe; to set foot in sth – einen Fuß in etw. setzen; to bend down – sich herunterbeugen; suspicious – misstrauisch; to take apart – auseinander nehmen

Paul's shoulder. "Someone's here to see you, Paul. Do you know her?"

Paul turns bright red the moment he sees me. He looks uncomfortable, not at all pleased to see me. He smiles **tensely** and looks from me to her, to me again. Then he **finds his tongue**. "Hello, Olli!"

Miss Pretty and I stare at him: we both want to know what's going on here.

"Linda, this is Olli. – And this is Linda." He **indicates** Miss Pretty, as if anybody else around here could be called Linda. "A ..." Paul **grinds to a halt**, honest Paul, "... my girlfriend."

The brats tear the basket out of my hands and disappear into the house with it.

Who cares? I couldn't hold onto it anymore. I've gone all weak. And because my knees are going **wobbly,** and because I don't want to play the main role in a bad film and **faint** right here in front of Linda, I try to leave as quickly as possible. "Nice to meet you," I say, or: "I just wanted to bring something round for the kids ...!" No idea. I mutter something like that – any old rubbish – and then I run down Bond Street, my Bond Street, which all of a sudden now belongs to Linda!

---

tense – angespannt; to find one's tongue – die Sprache wiederfinden; to indicate – zeigen;
to grind to a halt – ins Stocken geraten; who cares? – egal!; wobbly – wacklig; to faint – ohnmächtig werden

Picnic in Hell

She wants to have a birthday picnic! With the whole *family*! That means me, Robert, the left and right hand of the devil, and Paul. Paul belongs to my family. That's why I'll always have to keep meeting him, even though I never want to see him again.

"I can't!"

Mum looks at me, her eyebrows raised. Pure **astonishment**. "You can't come to my birthday party?"

"I can't come to your birthday party if that gorilla family is going to be there!"

Now she doesn't understand a thing. "Oh, right! So now he's back to being a gorilla again, is he?"

"Not just now. He never stopped being a gorilla. Especially his stupid children!"

Mum angrily cuts her toast into small pieces. "Great, Olli, but I just don't get it. First you think everything's terrible, you're utterly negative and you don't want to know. Then, all of sudden, that seems to **vanish into thin air**, you're as sweet as sugar and

---

astonishment – Erstaunen; to vanish into thin air – sich in Luft auflösen

you even jump at the chance of babysitting at gorilla's place. And now, whoosh, everything's the other way around again. Are you out of your mind or something? What's the matter with you?"

I really don't want to talk about it, not at all. I know perfectly well that she can't understand me because she has no idea that everything is to do with that bonehead Paul. My God, that **knocked me for six**! Paul has a girlfriend. He kissed me even though he has a girlfriend.

Babsi got really **worked up** about it. "And then he was too much of a **coward** to even tell you!"

Anna was so disappointed by Prince Charming she almost cried. "We can do without things like that, Olli," she'd whispered. "Only heroes are good enough for us."

Carla was as cool as ever. She was probably thinking to herself that she'd known all along that it would turn out like this. Even before I got to know Paul. Probably even at her own birth. But she didn't say anything. She just put her arm around my shoulders. The girls are the way they are, but when one of us is feeling bad, they all make an effort to behave **appropriately**. No **reproaches**, no lectures, no I-told-you-so comments.

---

to knock sb for six – jmdn. umhauen; worked up – aufgeregt; coward – Feigling; appropriate – passend/entsprechend; reproach – Vorwurf

All I could think was that he doesn't love me. Paul doesn't love me, Paul loves Linda. It's over. My happiness has **crumbled**. No, it's been **shattered**, blown up, destroyed, **obliterated**. I got a kiss from my Prince Charming. Just one. "Never again. I'll never kiss anyone again. It can never be like it was with Paul ever again. I'm going to become a nun!"

ABC tried to console me and talk me out of the nun idea, but I was absolutely **determined**. I would pay for the tragic events with my suffering, pacing up and down the **convent's** corridors with a shaved head and coarse hands from polishing the wooden floorboards, just suffering.

I lay awake in bed that night and stared at the ceiling. I wanted to stare for as long as it took until Paul's face stopped appearing, but it didn't go away. It was always there. *Time **heals** all wounds*. **A likely story**! This saying doesn't apply to me, that's for sure. I'll go to the convent with a deep wound in my heart, and it will never heal.

"And now she expects me to sit next to Paul on a chequered blanket having a picnic, waving sparklers, singing *Happy Birthday* and pretending

---

to crumble – zerbröckeln; to shatter – zerplatzen;
to obliterate – vernichten; determined – entschlossen;
convent – Frauenkloster; to heal – heilen;
A likely story! – Von wegen!/Denkste!

nothing has happened!" Of course, I have to tell ABC about this latest **blow below the belt** straightaway.

Anna, Babsi and Carla stare at me and think about the situation for a second.

"You can only go if you're strong enough to be cool and give him the cold shoulder. In every respect," thinks Carla.

No chance. I can't do that. Not as long as his face keeps appearing on my ceiling.

"But she can't just not go to her mum's birthday party!" objects Anna. **Addicted** to harmony! She's right, but she didn't have to say it.

All of a sudden, Babsi breaks into a huge, red-lipped smile. "Of course, you'll go, Olli!"

Horror. "No, I won't!"

Babsi continues grinning, **undeterred** by my vehement refusal. "You will. And you'll go with *your* boyfriend!"

I look at the others. Do they get what Babsi is on about? "But I don't have a boyfriend, and I don't want one either!"

Babsi nods. "That's what it looks like at the moment. But let me deal with that. You can rely on good old Babsi!"

---

blow below the belt – Schlag unterhalb der Gürtellinie; addicted – süchtig; undeterred – unerschrocken

The sun is shining brightly on Mum's birthday. It could have rained. Then I wouldn't have had to **put up** with all this rubbish. But, of course, the sun is shining.

Mum is shining even more than the sun as she gets into the gorilla's family minibus in the ancient flowery dress that some great-grandma of hers wore in the 20s to dance the Charleston. The **neckline** is far too low for her. Maybe her great-grandma was **built** somewhat differently, but Mum and I aren't like that. Mum's **solution** is to stick a huge flower in the neckline. Her **ridiculously** romantic mood and the whole revolting happiness of it all makes me feel utterly sick.

I clamber into the minibus with nothing but contempt, and I don't even deign to glance at Paul. I sit down behind him and the brats in the second row.

"'aulandolli, 'aulandolli," they shout **fittingly**, as sensitive as ever.

After the gorilla has kissed Mum at length to wish her happy birthday, we set off. I can tell Paul keeps turning around to me, but I just stare **stubbornly** out of the window, as if I've never seen a grey city passing me by from a car.

"You can play the same game as him. Just as

---

to put up with sth – etw. aushalten; neckline – Ausschnitt; built – gebaut; solution – Lösung; ridiculous – lächerlich; fittingly – passenderweise; stubborn – stur

you've settled down to your lovely picnic, your boyfriend turns up. That'll knock Paul for six!" Babsi has it all planned.

And I'm sticking to the plan. When Mum and the gorilla start singing *we're going for a picnic, what a lot of fun, we're going for a picnic, in the sun*, my **facial features** almost **derail**. They really stop at nothing. Sometimes, when I peer out to the front, I catch a glimpse of Paul's neck. If I didn't hate him so much, I would touch it, it looks so soft where the **hairline** is. But I hate him and wouldn't dream of touching him.

Mum and Robert spread out the chequered (!) picnic blanket on a huge **lawn** in the park, laughing at how the blanket **puffs up** as they shake it out. What's so funny about that?

The left and right hand of the devil are allowed to take their **nappies** off. "So they can get a bit of air," claims Robert.

Now the two of them are running around the blanket, nappyless. "'icnic, 'icnic!"

Paul is sitting on the lawn, plucking **tufts of grass** and tossing them to one side. He doesn't look particularly happy about being here, I have to say. But I wouldn't be in his position either.

---

facial features – Gesichtszüge; to derail – entgleisen; hairline – Haaransatz; lawn – Rasen; to puff up – aufblähen; nappy – Windel; tuft of grass – Grasbüschel

I make an effort. I don't want to make such a **grumpy** impression as him. I pretend everything's great, and I help Mum set out the thousands of **delicacies**.

"It took me days to cook this," she declares proudly.

They laugh again. No idea why.

The gorilla takes Paul's trumpet case out of the car and waves over to his **sullen** son. "Look, Paul. I thought you could play Christie something!"

Christie – urgh!

Paul's face darkens. He waves his hand dismissively and shakes his head.

It seems the twins have **inherited** their sensitivity from the gorilla. He won't let go of his suggestion. He probably thinks Paul's mood will **improve** if he plays. Undeterred, he unpacks the trumpet, presses it into Paul's grassy-green hands and whispers to him, loud enough for everyone to hear, "Come on, for her birthday!"

Paul has no other choice. He **listlessly** plays *Happy Birthday* – a bit too fast – and everybody joins in singing. Even me because it's not Mum's fault that Paul and I hate each other.

Passers-by in the park stop and **poignantly** ap-

---

grumpy – griesgrämig; delicacy – Köstlichkeit;
sullen – missmutig; to inherit – erben; to improve – verbessern;
listless – lustlos; passer-by – Passant; poignant – ergreifend

plaud this perfect family. Don't bother! It's all just a lie!

"So, **dig in**!" Mum opens the buffet and is a bit grumpy because the devil's hands run right across the blanket, through the **pâté** and into the noodle salad. "Fritz, Franz, no … Robert, say something!"

Robert gradually pulls his brats out of the food and just smiles. Mum wrinkles her brow. Then we start eating – all of us except Paul. He just **prods** his noodle salad listlessly. Occasionally, he looks up to me, but I don't look at him. I let him stew. Now would be a good point for *my* boyfriend to turn up, I think.

"But not Lubo!" I told Babsi. "No way!"

Babsi immediately waved her hand in dismissal. "Never. It would be a shame to **waste** someone like Lubo on this!"

The devil's hands set off to destroy the world around us. Mum is getting slightly hysterical because she has sat down on an **anthill,** and the horrible little creatures have courageously set about **overcoming** the **obstacle**. They're crawling all over her. I can't eat anymore because, as always, all the **wasps** are coming to me, and to me only. So we try to fight off the insects of this world and don't **pay**

---

dig in – hau(t) rein; pâté – Pastete; to prod – stochern;
to waste – verschwenden; anthill – Ameisenhaufen;
to overcome – überwinden; obstacle – Hindernis; wasp – Wespe

any **attention** to what the brats are doing, until Paul suddenly shouts, "Fritz, Franz, get out of the water!"

In typical brat style, they've managed to find the **first available** deadly **trap** and are standing up to their bellies in the pond, wading ever deeper. Are they stupid or what? Are they just going to keep wading out until they **drown**?

We all run off, shouting our heads off. Paul and I jump into the water fully clothed and head towards the children, who slowly **lose their footing**. The gorilla and Mum stand on the **bank** of the pond, waving their arms frantically, which is of absolutely no help whatsoever – in case they didn't notice it themselves. Paul and I each manage to grab one of the brats.

"Are you two out of your mind? Have you gone crazy?" Paul shouts, really worked up.

The children kick out their legs, splashing like mad and shouting, "'queaky duck, 'queaky duck …!" which is a **reference** to a small family of ducks which the brats obviously took to be **squeaky ducks**. That's just the way they are.

We pass on the soaking wet hands of the devil to

---

to pay attention – aufpassen; first available – nächstbeste; trap – Falle; to drown – ertrinken; to lose one's footing – seinen Halt verlieren; bank – Ufer; reference – Anspielung; squeaky duck – Quietschente

Mum and the gorilla. They immediately wrap them in towels, lovingly rub them dry and gently **scold** them in typical gorilla style. Hello? I'm wet, too! I sit down on the grass. The sun can dry me in peace and quiet.

But the peace and quiet doesn't last long. Paul sits down next to me. "Thanks," he says, looking at me. I look straight ahead. What was I supposed to do, let his stupid brothers drown?

"I have to talk to you, Olli!"

I look away. The body language is clear: *But I don't have to talk to you.*

But it makes no difference to Paul. "I just wanted to say, when we … when we kissed … it just happened!"

Now he's going to say he's sorry. He's going to **ruin** the one and only kiss I have.

"I didn't want to hurt you!"

My eyes fill up with tears. He mustn't see them. Ever.

"I don't usually do things like that. Honest. That kiss really knocked me for six. First of all I had to **sort** things **out** … Do you know what I mean?"

At least it knocked him for six. Or is he just trying to **butter** me **up** again? The alarm bells would be ringing if Carla were here!

---

to scold – ausschimpfen; to ruin – verderben; to sort sth out – etw. klären; to butter sb up – jmdn. einwickeln

"Look at me!"

I try to think clearly, but I can't. I have to look at him. What else can I do?

"I've told Linda it's over!"

Whaaaat? Because of me? Oh no, oh God, this can't be true! Paul, my …

"*Hola, tesoro*, it's me, your beloved **darling**!" Jorge is standing in front of us, and before I know what's going on, he bends down and kisses me. Right on the mouth. Now of all times! Jorge of all people!

I turn away to stop him from kissing me more, and I'm just about to explain everything to Paul when I think: but how? What am I meant to say? "We organised this to make you …!" He'll think I'm stupid.

Jorge sits down coolly between me and Paul and puts his arm around me. "Did you have a nice party, sweetheart?" he asks, holding me firmly. "Sorry, I'm so late. I guess this is Paul, that friend of yours." He turns to Paul and holds out his hand for a buddy **handshake**. "Chorche, Olli's lover!"

Paul gets to his feet and wipes his hands on his wet trousers. He's gone really **pale**. He looks at me hurt, turns and leaves.

"Paul, I can explain everything!" I call after him.

But Paul doesn't want to have anything ex-

---

darling – Schatz; handshake – Handschlag; pale – blass

plained. I can understand that: I felt the same until just now. But Paul just leaves. **Soaked to the skin**, just as he is.

I stare at Jorge, thinking about the **vile language** I'm about to use on him. Why did Babsi have to choose him of all people?

Then Mum and Robert start arguing. Mum shouts across the entire lawn at him. And when she shouts, no eye stays dry. "It can't go on like this! How can anyone put up with the way you **pamper** those brats? Of course, they just do what they want!"

Once again all the passers-by stop and look, but this time no one applauds. The perfect family is shattered again.

"Christie, calm down. That's my thing, don't you think?" The gorilla hasn't **grasped** yet that Mum's in a rage, and when she's like that, you shouldn't try to **reason** with her.

"If that's so, then it can be your thing **as far as I'm concerned**. I can't put up with it any longer. And don't call me Christie!" shouts Mum. Then she turns around and leaves as well.

---

to be soaked to the skin – bis auf die Haut nass sein;
to use vile language on sb – jmdn. wüst beschimpfen;
to pamper – verhätscheln; to grasp – begreifen;
to reason with sb – vernünftig mit jmdm. reden;
as far as I'm concerned – meinetwegen

The gorilla watches her go. He looks so sad, I almost feel sorry for him. Then he takes his devil's hands and disappears.

Jorge **launches himself at** the picnic while I remain sitting on the grass in a state of shock. So Paul **dumped** Miss Pretty Linda for me. Theoretically everything would be fine if Jorge hadn't turned up. And I'll never be able to explain that to Paul, because he'll think I'm stupid. And can it be that Mum just dumped the gor... I mean, Robert?

"Great atmosphere here, sweetheart!" Jorge calls over to me with his mouth full. I finally manage to get to my feet and shout back at him with all my **fury**, "Don't call me sweetheart, **slimeball**!"

---

to launch oneself at sth – sich auf etw. stürzen; to dump sb – jmdn. verlassen; fury – Wut; slimeball – Schleimbeutel

ABC in the Schoolyard

"Poor Olli, so near and yet so far." Anna is sitting in the middle of a concrete table tennis table in the schoolyard, her face **overcome with remorse**. "I mean, what does he think about her now?"

"He thinks that Olli has a boyfriend. That's no bad thing. He **was already taken** as well!" Babsi is sitting on the left, **dangling her feet** from the table, admiring her new sandals. Not in the best of moods.

"No, no!" objects Anna. "He thinks that Olli was standing in front of his front door with an anti-stress basket and was obviously trying to win him over. That made him end things with Linda, who he's known since he was in a **pram** ..."

"How do you know that?" snaps Babsi.

"I'm just guessing."

"It's called a worst-case scenario." Carla is cleaning her glasses to Anna's right. "That's what happens when people **meddle** in things."

---

overcome with remorse – zerknirscht;
to be already taken – schon vergeben sein;
to dangle one's feet – mit den Füßen baumeln;
pram – Kinderwagen; to meddle – sich einmischen

Babsi jumps down from the table and plants herself in front of Carla, absolutely **livid**. "I know perfectly well what you're trying to say. The message is loud and clear. But you're wrong." She pokes her finger with its long nail into Carla's chest, and Carla backs off in the face of such raw aggression. "Am I right or am I right when I say we were **unanimous**? We all thought it was a good idea. We **voted** on it and chose Jorge!"

"That's true, Carla!" butts in Anna.

Carla waves her hand dismissively. "Alright, alright. It's still our fault that everything's ruined anyway."

Babsi paces nervously to and fro in front of the table tennis table.

"Maybe indirectly, but Olli knew about the plan and she agreed to it. So that makes Olli just as guilty as us."

Carla sighs. "If that makes it any better!"

"It makes no difference now. The fresh romance has been **nipped in the bud**." Anna's bottom lip wobbles. "And that's so sad!"

Carla rolls her eyes. "Lord above, it's not as bad as all that. Think about all the things Olli won't have to put up with now: the first arguments about nothing in particular, the disappointments, getting

---

livid – wütend; unanimous – einstimmig; to vote – abstimmen; to nip sth in the bud – etw. im Keim ersticken

bored with each another, the first **infidelity**, the deep wounds and the inevitable end of it all!"

"But also the first … er … experiences of being with someone, holding hands in a dark cinema, spending hours with each other, growing in trust, growing together, getting engaged …!"

"ANNA!" shriek Carla and Babsi both together.

"Yes? What are you shouting about?"

Babsi sits back down in her place, shaking her head. "There's one thing we can say for sure: it was a real **cock-up**. And it's hardly a miracle that Olli is now lying in bed feeling ill and never wants to get up again!"

"*Hola, tesoro!*" As ever, Jorge appears **out of nowhere** and sticks out his broad Argentinian lips to his beloved Babsi. "I've come for my **reward**!"

Babsi **shrinks back**, startled, and taps her forehead with her finger. "You must have **lost your marbles**. You ruined everything!"

Jorge swings himself up onto the table tennis table and sits down close next to her.

Babsi backs off.

Jorge slips closer. "I did what you asked. The guy thought I was Olli's boyfriend. So I get a kiss!"

---

infidelity – Untreue; cock-up (ugs.) – Schlamassel;
out of nowhere – aus dem Nichts; reward – Belohnung;
to shrink back – zurückweichen;
to lose one's marbles – den Verstand verlieren

"If he's right, then he's right," says Anna seriously.

Carla can't help smiling.

Babsi jumps off the table tennis table. "You guys are the pits. Now you're all acting as if I did this on my own." She storms off.

Jorge goes after her. "A deal is a deal, *tesoro*. A kiss for your hero!"

Babsi stops in her tracks, turns around to him and **barks**, "But not here, in the middle of the schoolyard, you **moron**!" Then she disappears into the school building.

"Did you know that you can get **caries** through a kiss?" Carla asks Anna and follows Babsi.

---

to bark at sb – jmdn. anschnauzen; moron – Blödmann; caries – Karies

Lovesick

We're lying in bed together. It's warmer with the two of us. We can talk about everything. You're not left alone with all your thoughts, going around in endless circles and never getting anywhere. We haven't done this for a long time, Mum and I, lying in bed together. In the middle of the day. The times we have done it was when one of us was feeling bad and the other one consoled her. Today we're both down, right at **rock-bottom**. We're **lovesick**. So badly lovesick that Mum hasn't turned around the **sign** which some 18th-century flower-seller in England painted and which now hangs on the shop door. That's why the side facing out says *Closed*. And that's why I'm not in school talking everything through with ABC in the break. I just couldn't face it. I'm happy that I've finally told Mum everything. I'm happy that she knows I'm in love with her lover's son. Ex-lover, I should say.

Mum gives a melancholic smile. "It's a funny **coincidence**, isn't it?"

---

rock-bottom – ganz unten; to be lovesick – Liebeskummer haben; sign – Schild; coincidence – Zufall

Very funny. I nod.

"Just imagine if I'd have married Robert. Then you'd suddenly be in love with your brother." Mum has to laugh.

"Stepbrother!" I object.

Mum promptly falls silent because she notices how serious I am, and because she remembers that it's hardly looking like wedding bells between her and Robert. We sigh and sip our tea.

The telephone rings for the hundredth time. Needless to say, it's Robert again, and Mum just leaves him to talk into the **answerphone**. "Christieeee! Come on, answer the phone! Please. Let's talk. You can reach me at the youth centre for the next two hours, then I'll be at home. Please call. I miss you!"

I look at Mum out of the corner of my eye. She's squeezing her lips together so tightly that they've turned from red to white. She's not cool, not at all, even if it's meant to look like that.

"At least yours calls," I say, blowing into my cup of tea.

"Yours can't call. It's your turn now."

She's right really, but there's **no point**, I know that with my eyes closed. It was too hard yesterday. "I expect he's run straight back to Linda and is having a good cry on her big boobs."

---

answerphone – Anrufbeantworter; no point – keinen Sinn

"Why shouldn't he? After all, he thinks you're with that other boy … What's he called?"

"Chorche!" I scrape his name out of my throat.

"Ch… ch… ch...!" Mum is unable to pronounce his name correctly.

We burst out laughing. They're mad, the Argentinians!

I put my tea down, pull the **covers** up under my nose and stare at the ceiling. Paul is still there. Hello, Paul! "What am I supposed to do? You're experienced, Mum! Come on, give me a tip!"

Mum slips under the covers as well. I wonder if she can see Robert's face. Maybe he's stuck up there next to Paul, looking down at us sadly. "You should at least try to explain it to him! You haven't got anything to lose."

She can talk. How am I meant to explain it to Paul?

"Tell him the way it was."

The phone rings. Paul perhaps? "*Hello, Olli, answer the phone. Let's talk. Maybe it's all just a stupid* ***misunderstanding.***"

No. It's Robert again. He says that there's nothing he can do but to keep calling, and so on and so forth.

Mum has tears in her eyes, and it's about time for

---

covers – Bettdecke;
misunderstanding – Missverständnis

me to **exercise my authority**. Even though gorilla-man Robert **can go take a running jump** as far as I'm concerned. "Why don't you answer the phone? Why don't you talk to him? You have this really tiny problem with the brats, and you've already **thrown in the towel**." I have to pour myself another tea.

"Your problem with Paul isn't exactly **earth-shattering**. Things like that can be cleared up easily enough, and then it's over!" Mum hits back.

We both stare straight ahead with a grim expression on our faces. Then we both sigh.

"Why do I always ruin everything?" Mother.

"Why did I get involved in such a stupid mess?" Daughter.

Silence.

"What if he doesn't want to talk to me?" I whisper.

"What if he doesn't want someone who shouts around?" whispers Mum.

We're both just scared. I always used to think that when you get as old as Mum, you sort things out differently because you've **been through** things

---

to exercise one's authority – ein Machtwort sprechen;
he/she can go take a running jump! –
er/sie kann mir gestohlen bleiben!;
to throw in the towel – das Handtuch werfen; earth-shattering – weltbewegend; to be through sth – etw. durchmachen

a hundred times. But it's not true. Even when you're old, you're still scared of love.

All of a sudden, Mum sits up in bed. She looks like she's just had an idea, and that it wasn't a bad one.

"Paul's got his church concert today."

I nod. So what?

"Let's go there. Together. And **make up with** our men." Mum is thrilled.

"I don't know. You can go …"

Mum takes my hands, squeezes them tight and looks at me with a **sparkle** in her eyes. "We're going together. Together we're strong. You'll see. It'll all work out!"

By the afternoon Robert had called about forty thousand times.

Mum and I have worked out what we were going to do precisely: she'll just sit down next to Robert. Surprise! They'll listen to the concert together, and they'll be holding hands again by the second **movement** at the latest.

"And I'll explain everything to him after the concert. That it's none of my business how he **brings up** his children, but that I should be allowed to **ex-**

---

to make up with sb – sich mit jmdm. versöhnen;
sparkle – Funkeln; movement – Satz; to bring up – erziehen;
to express an opinion – seine Meinung äußern

press my opinion about it. I spend so much time with those …"

"… brats!"

"Don't you think?"

Mum continues talking non-stop. She's more excited than a bee round a honeypot. I, on the other hand, feel **uneasy**. What am I meant to say? And above all: what will he say? I have to clear this up before the concert, for sure. Then he can **think** everything **through** while he plays. Like whether he actually believes me that I'm not like that, that I never normally do such stupid things. I was just so hurt. People do stupid things when they're hurt, surely he'll understand that, won't he? He'll play his trumpet, I'll listen to him, and the whole time we'll look at each other deeper and deeper, until our glances become bound and **welded together** for ever. Perhaps! Hopefully! Inevitably!

On the way to the church Mum talks nineteen to the dozen. She forgets to pay attention to where we're going, and we get horribly lost. We end up getting to the church just before the doors close.

"Shit," hisses Mum **under her breath**, but the naughty word **echoes** through the church, bouncing off the walls and into the ears of all those pre-

---

uneasy – beklommen; to think sth through – etw. durchdenken; to weld sth together – etw. zusammenschweißen; under one's breath – leise vor sich hin; to echo – hallen

sent. Mum turns bright red and apologetically waves the **heel** which has come off her shoe.

But that's still no reason to say 'shit' in a church, think the people in the audience and punish her with looks of contempt. Only Robert doesn't. He jumps up from his seat, a beaming smile on his face, and **embraces** Mum. It looks like they'll be holding hands from the very beginning then, whereas my plan is **backfiring** already. There's no way I can speak to Paul beforehand. The concert is about to begin, any second now.

I squeeze my way through to some complete strangers. I don't want to sit next to Robert and Mum while they whisper excitedly through the concert and everyone around them hisses "*Sshh!*" because of them. Besides, the left and right hand of the devil are sitting right next to them. Of course, the gorilla has taken them with him, although he knows that they'll completely **flip out** after the first minute and turn the entire church on its head. No, really, I'd rather sit a little bit behind them.

Silence.

I **lean back** and look at the church ceiling, which seems to be infinitely far away. What now? A new

---

heel – Absatz; to embrace sb – jmdn. umarmen;
to backfire – nach hinten losgehen;
to flip out – ausrasten;
to lean back – zurücklehnen

plan? There's only one option: I'll have to talk to Paul after the concert.

Thunderous applause.

The orchestra comes in, all dressed in black. It couldn't be more ceremonious. Where's Paul? I can't see him! Why does the Biggest Man in the World always have to sit in front of me? Why can't he just stay at home when I go to a concert or the cinema? The Biggest Man in the World always goes where I go.

But then I spot him. Paul in a **suit**. With his freckles. Unbelievable. The Trumpeting Prince! I only have eyes for him. For the entire concert. I watch every single move he makes. The way he blows the trumpet and always turns the page of his music at the right time. The way he's so concentrated. He never looks up. Not once. And so he doesn't see me either. The way he listens with his eyes closed when the others are playing and he's not. The way he steps forward at one point because he's got a solo. No, a duet. Another trumpeter comes forward. A blonde girl with huge boobs and a really low neckline – why doesn't Linda just perform **naked**? Oh, so it's like that! So I guessed right. I sink back into my **pew** and am happy that the Biggest Man in the World is always with me.

Mum turns around and shakes her head at me

---

suit – Anzug; naked – nackt; pew – Kirchenbank

slightly. What's she trying to say? That it doesn't **necessarily** mean anything? She can shake her head: she's sitting there with her beloved gorilla, the two sweet little brats between them, their cheeks **rosy** with excitement, sitting perfectly still, like they've been **glued down**. A picture of perfect happiness. Whereas I have to watch on as Paul **fervently** plays his trumpet with a big-breasted – maybe they're not real? – Barbie doll. I stare at my shoes. I can't bear to look anymore.

"He could hardly not turn up to the concert just because he dumped Linda!" Mum has squeezed in next to me, and the people in my pew are giving us furious looks because there wasn't even room for me alone. We smile back at them **amiably**, and Mum gives me an **encouraging** nod and hobbles back to her seat without her heel.

Could she be right? I watch Paul and Linda carefully. They're both really **wrapped up** in their music and if I could unplug my ears from **jealousy**, then I'd have to admit, it sounds really great. Maybe Mum really is right? The orchestra could never have found a **replacement** either for him or

---

not necessarily – nicht unbedingt; rosy – rosig;
to glue down – festkleben; fervent – inbrünstig;
amiable – freundlich; encouraging – aufmunternd;
wrapped up – vertieft; jealousy – Eifersucht;
replacement – Ersatz

for her at such short notice. So they had to **bite the bullet**, **grin and bear it** and perform together. That's show business for you. Yes, Mum's right.

The orchestra is rewarded by thunderous applause. Paul and Linda keep having to step forward to **take a bow**. They don't bow hand in hand, something I take as being a good sign. While the audience continues clapping, I discreetly **sneak** over to the door where Paul and Linda keep going **backstage**.

The whole orchestra is **gathered** backstage, talking excitedly about mistakes that came up and passages which didn't go so well. I **huddle** in the corner next to a **double bass** because I shouldn't be here, and wait for Paul. At last the audience settles down, and Paul and Linda appear backstage. They're both completely beside themselves, which I can understand after all that applause. Paul drops into an old armchair, sinking down so low that all I can see are his hands resting on the **armrests** – presumably to stop him from sinking into the armchair for ever. Now is the time to make my **entrance**! He won't be able to get out of that arm-

---

to bite the bullet – in den sauren Apfel beißen;
to grin and bear it – gute Miene zum bösen Spiel machen;
to take a bow – sich verbeugen; to sneak – schleichen;
backstage – hinter die/der Bühne; to gather – sich versammeln;
to huddle – sich drücken; double bass – Kontrabass;
armrest – Armlehne; entrance – Auftritt

chair so quickly. He'll have to listen to me. OK, go for it.

But just as I'm about to go over, Linda appears and bends down to Paul – so low that he definitely sees everything that's being **laboriously** held together by her **wafer-thin** dress. As she leans over, she coquettishly lifts up one leg. I hear Paul laugh.

Each sound is like a **dagger** in my heart, **piercing** me deeper and deeper with each blow. Mum wasn't right. Paul jumped right back into Linda's arms. Paul is not who I thought he was. He takes what he can get his hands on, and I won't play that game, not me. As much as it hurts, I am not **available**. And that's that!

I slip quietly out of the backstage room into the church. It's now empty, and there's no trace of the concert that has just taken place here. I look up at the church ceiling, which is so far away and seems to be disappearing more and more into the distance.

"Olliolliolliolliolli!" The left and right hand of the devil are back to their old ways again, and I quickly **wipe away** my tears. I don't want to spoil their mood, the whole happy family!

---

laborious – mühsam; wafer-thin – hauchdünn; dagger – Dolch; to pierce – durchstechen; to be available – zur Verfügung stehen; to wipe away – abwischen

Lubo's Posse

Lubo's boathouse is at 26 Waterway Road, a **rickety** blue **hut** hidden behind thick undergrowth, with a **jetty** stretching out into the lake.

After the disaster in the church I immediately had to inform ABC. Only I didn't want to go and eat ice-cream with them, even though they were now **reconciled**. That's all I needed! It was hard enough just going on being Olli, and to grasp that the earth was still turning, and that at some point I would probably either feel hungry or think about things like the weather or my next pocket money. At the moment I just feel empty. I can't think. I just have this **dull**, **numb** feeling.

"What a disaster!" I said on the phone, and these words **triggered** the girls **off** to move with **supersonic speed**.

Barely half an hour later they were standing on my doorstep.

---

rickety – klapperig; hut – Hütte; jetty – Steg;
reconciled – versöhnt; dull – dumpf; numb – klamm;
to trigger sth off – etw. auslösen;
supersonic speed – Überschallgeschwindigkeit

"You know what they say, Olli: if you don't want it, you've probably already got it. Someone who rushes back into the arms of his ex … You can do without guys like that!"

I ask myself if Babsi would be quite as tough if she were in my position. But then she wouldn't be Babsi. Everybody's different.

"Guys like that just can't be alone. He's always looking for **recognition** from a woman who tells him he's really great, the best man ever, with the biggest ever **dick**!"

"Carla!" squealed Anna.

"It's true!" said Carla, agreeing with Babsi in this matter. That must surely tell me something.

They're probably right. It doesn't seem to make any difference to Paul who's at his side, just as long as someone's there, just as long as he's not single. Not exactly the sort of **behaviour** you'd expect from Prince Charming.

Anna puts her arm through mine. "I know how Olli's feeling!"

"How?" asked Babsi.

No one would normally respond to a **jibe** like this, but, unfortunately, Anna doesn't even realise it's a jibe. "I can **empathize** with her! If you think

---

recognition – Anerkennung; dick (ugs.) – Schwanz/Penis; behaviour – Benehmen; jibe – Stichelei; to empathize – sich in jmdn. einfühlen

you've found your Prince Charming all of a sudden, it's difficult to let him go."

Thanks, Anna. Could be.

Of course, it was Babsi, as ever, who knew exactly what to do. "Hey, haven't you got someone else **up your sleeve**?"

I didn't know what she was on about because I was busy doing the **Mourning**-for-Paul routine. The other two nodded meaningfully.

"The most **sought-after** guy in school fancies you," Anna explained to me with a trace of **wistfulness** in her voice. She wouldn't say no to kissing him, not at all, maybe even with her you-know-what.

"Can't we forget about boys for a while?" moaned Carla.

Needless to say, Babsi had no intention of doing so. "What day does it happen to be today?" she asked us with a grin.

"Friday," we all answered at once.

"And who meets up at the lake every Friday?"

"Lubo!"

That's why we're on our way there now.

"No, I don't want anything from Lubo!" I tried to explain to Babsi.

---

to have sth up one's sleeve – etw. auf Lager haben; mourning – Trauer; sought-after – begehrt; wistfulness – Wehmut

But she's quite sure that when I see Lubo again, I'll soon forget Paul.

"But then I'd be doing the same as him!" I protested.

"Old love never dies!" she **claimed**, touching up her lipstick and pushing us off. "And if you don't want anything from him – you know where I am. OK?"

Now we're standing in front of the old fence which runs around the house at the lake. There is a gate, but it's locked, and there's no bell as far as the eye can see.

"Are Lubo's parents rich enough to **afford** a lake-side house?" asks Anna.

Babsi pulls herself up the gate and swings a leg over. "It doesn't belong to Lubo's parents."

"So who does it belong to then?" asks Anna, eyes wide with horror.

"Some people. But they're never here," replies Babsi as she jumps down on the other side of the gate into the stranger's **property**.

Carla follows her.

"You're not seriously trying to tell me we're **breaking and entering** into a complete stranger's house?"

---

to claim – behaupten; to afford sth – sich etw. leisten; property – Grundstück; to break and enter – einbrechen

"The owners aren't here, Anna, didn't you hear that?" says Carla, jumping down to Babsi.

Now it's my turn. "Come one, Anna, it's OK!" I try to **reassur**e her.

Anna shakes her head **fiercely** – I might have guessed she would do this. "Nothing is OK!" she whines. "I don't do things like this. It's not allowed!"

The three of us try to talk her into joining us on the other side of the fence. Can't she smell the **barbecue**? Can't she hear the guitar? The gentle **lapping** of the cool water?

"But it's not allowed!" says Anna, **digging in her heels**.

We decide that it's her own fault if she doesn't want to join us. She can either wait for us or go home. We head over to the others at the waterside.

"Hey! You can't just leave me here on my own!" she shouts after us. But we can.

As I happen to glance over my shoulder, I see Anna **draped** over the gate, trying to swing her leg over. She doesn't do things like that often, our Anna.

We fight our way along the **overgrown** path, and it really looks like no one has been here for years. There's a long jetty stretching out into the water di-

---

to reassure sb – jmdn. beruhigen; fierce – wild; barbecue – Grill; lapping – Plätschern; to dig in your heels – stur bleiben; to drape – herabhängen; overgrown – überwuchert

rectly from the boathouse. A few people are sitting on it or lying around: two of them are playing the guitar and singing, one is grilling sausages on sticks over a fire, others are in the water, others are asleep. It all looks very **homely**, I have to say.

"We should have brought something with us," I whisper to ABC.

"Did he invite you or didn't he?" asks Babsi in a loud voice, and it doesn't seem to **occur to** her that that's exactly the point: he invited *me*, not me and three others. Without thinking about it, Babsi goes down to the jetty and we follow her like **geese**.

Lubo is just pulling himself out of the water, **wringing out** his wet hair, with nothing on except a pair of boxer shorts which are clinging to his skin. He's really good-looking. When he sees us, he grins and comes over to us. He goes right past ABC to me. "Hey, Olivia, what a surprise!" He doesn't seem to be bothered that the others have come, too. He just ignores them, completely and utterly. Then he puts his wet arm around my shoulder and **leads me off**.

"My friends came, too …" I start trying to explain.

"What do you want to drink?" he asks without listening to me.

---

homely – gemütlich; to occur to sb – jmdm. einfallen; geese (sing. goose) – Gänse; to wring out – auswringen; to lead sb off – jmdn. wegführen

I shrug my shoulders at ABC, but they wave me on: I shouldn't worry about them, they can look after themselves.

Only Anna calls after us, "Is it true that this place doesn't belong to your parents, Lubo?"

Lubo only hears what he wants to hear. That's why Anna doesn't get an answer and I get a coke, although I didn't ask for one. Lubo pulls a **bucket** out of the water where the bottles are being kept cool. "So, do you like it here?"

I'm standing on the jetty of a romantic blue boathouse listening to guitar music with an ice-cold coke in my hand, looking out over the green lake. Of course, I like it. Nobody wouldn't like it, unless you're called Anna. She's running around asking everyone who the property belongs to, and if they're not scared – don't they know that you can end up in prison for **trespassing**? – trying not to look at the girls' naked breasts – they're all topless! She keeps looking **anxiously** over to the entrance to see whether a masked **task force** with water cannons and truncheons is about to burst in.

Needless to say, Babsi **strips off** her clothes **without further ado**. Wearing no more than her sexy underwear, she's lying on her stomach in

---

bucket – Eimer; trespassing – Hausfriedensbruch;
anxious – besorgt; task force – Einsatzkommando;
to strip off – abstreifen; without further ado – ohne Weiteres

front of the guitar players, singing along with her high-pitched Marilyn-like voice.

Carla has sat down in the **shade**, fully clothed and wearing a pair of large, dark sunglasses, through which she can inconspicuously observe events. Everything that she regards with contempt.

"It's nice here," I reply in the end.

Lubo gently puts his hand on my back and directs me towards a blanket spread out at the front of the jetty. He lies down on it, **cranes** his face to the sun and pats the ground next to him. "Come here!"

There's something really **domineering** about him, and that's beginning to get on my nerves a bit. But still, I sit down next to him and give it some time. What's he going to do now? I expect he wants to know who I left him standing for in the school hall. I'd want to know if I were him.

But I'm not Lubo. He's not interested. He rolls onto his side, props his head up on his hand and looks at me out of one eye. He has to **squint** with the other one because of the sun. "Are you hungry, Olivia?" At least he's remembered my name.

"Everybody just calls me Olli!"

He smiles at me, good-looking Lubo, and I smile

---

shade – Schatten; to crane – recken;
domineering – bestimmend/herrschsüchtig;
to squint – die Augen zukneifen

back. What else am I supposed to do? I can't look at him grumpily. There's no reason to do that.

"I could go and get you a few sausages!"

That's really nice of him because it's back at last – the hunger which I thought had gone forever. I nod, and Lubo disappears over to the barbecue.

There are boats and ducks and **swans** on the lake. It's all unbelievably romantic.

"Olli, come on, admit it. We can't just break in like this!" Anna is standing next to me, looking pretty desperate, like a **hunted deer** or a **hare** in a trap.

I take her hand and look up at her. "Anna! Just sit down somewhere, get yourself something to drink and eat, let the sun shine on you, and stop worrying all the time. It's OK, really! They come here every Friday!"

Anna looks at me sceptically, has one more glance at the **enemy** behind her, and then admits defeat. "You accept full responsibility?"

"If you want!" I sigh.

Anna trudges off and looks for a place to sit down. Now I can finally just look at the ducks and the boats and think about Paul. Paul!

"Watch out! Here you go! Sausages for madam!"

---

swan – Schwan; hunted deer – gehetztes Reh; hare – Hase; enemy – Feind

Lubo has carefully arranged four sausages in a pool of **mustard** and ketchup, and has even added a few little flowers as decoration. Very **stylish**! He drops down next to me on the blanket and watches me eat without taking his eyes off me.

For some reason I find it extremely **unpleasant** when sausage fat and ketchup **oozes out** of the corner of my mouth while someone is looking at me. "Look somewhere else, it's embarrassing!" I demand with my mouth full.

Lubo grins from ear to ear and looks over to the lake. "What do you do apart from showing pornos at summer fêtes?"

The sausages are hot, and I have to try and breathe in as much cool air as possible through my teeth. I'm not in a position to talk, even if it's only small talk and is of no interest to anyone! "And you? Apart from hanging around on other people's property surrounded by girls?" I mumble.

Lubo looks at me really seriously, and all of a sudden, I have the sneaking suspicion that I've just **stirred up a hornets' nest** again, turning the knife in the wound. That's my speciality. I know nothing and always say exactly the wrong thing. "I **look after**

---

mustard – Senf; stylish – stilvoll;
unpleasant – unangenehm; to ooze out of sth – aus etw. tropfen;
to stir up a hornets' nest – in ein Wespennest stechen;
to look after sb – sich um jmdn. kümmern

my grandma. I live with her, and I have to take care of her a bit."

That knocks me for six. In reality, cool Lubo is a **geriatric nurse**? "And your parents?"

"They work abroad. Just for a few years **supposedly**. I was five when they said that!" He smiles at me uneasily. "But a few years is just a question of definition, I suppose."

I feel really sorry for him. It must be really awful if both parents aren't interested in you. "My dad disappeared as well." But I still have Mum. OK, right now she's in love with the gorilla, and there's going to be a lot of hassle. Things look bad for me, now that I don't want to have anything to do with the gorilla's son. But she's there. She shows an interest in my life. She loves me.

Two **barefooted** older girls come up **on tiptoe**, their naked boobs bouncing up and down. They've got bright white teeth, flowers in their hair and are absolutely perfect. "Hey, Lubomirowitsch, want to come for a swim with us?"

Lubo grins at them and waves them away. "I haven't got time right now!"

The girls look disappointed and eye me up from head to toe. What does their Lubomirowitsch want from a fully-dressed girl from the 8th Grade who's

---

geriatric nurse – Altenpfleger(in); supposedly – angeblich; barefooted – barfüßig; on tiptoe – auf Zehenspitzen

got ketchup oozing out of the corner of her mouth?

"Is your grandma ill?" I ask because I always think it's exciting when you find out things about people that you'd never have expected.

But all of a sudden, we're **torn out** of our idyllic setting by a startling cry for help. "Oh no, they're here! I knew it. Help! We're going to end up in prison! They're here, they're here!" Anna. She's standing there, bright red in the face, pointing behind her at an elderly couple who have no idea what's going on.

The two of them are staring in amazement at the people who have **made themselves at home** on their property.

Lubo jumps up and pulls me with him. "Everybody scram!" he shouts, and everyone immediately wakes up and starts to run off.

I see Babsi frantically gathering her clothes together, Carla, who stands up **as cool as a cucumber** and strolls off; and Anna, who seems to be **rooted to the spot**, screaming.

Lubo pulls me along the jetty towards the water. "Come on, Olli, quickly!"

---

to tear out – ausreißen;
to make oneself at home – es sich gemütlich machen;
as cool as a cucumber – mit einem kühlen Kopf;
to be rooted to the spot – wie angewurzelt dastehen

I try to persuade Anna to escape. "Anna, run!" I cry. After all, I did accept full responsibility for the situation.

All of a sudden, Lubo jumps into the water holding my hand so tightly that I can only jump with him, fully clothed, but **what the hell**. I follow Lubo along the lakeside underwater and feel like Winnetou with a knife **clenched** between my teeth. Any moment now we'll make a straw out of a **reed**, so that we can swim underwater without being seen, and we'll thank Manitu for always protecting us with his mighty hand.

We swim to the **surface** amongst the thick reeds of the neighbouring house. Heads only at first.

Lubo smiles at me, his eyes shining, and he takes my hands. "You're just great!" he says softly and kisses me.

He kisses differently from Paul. It's like how he didn't listen a few moments ago. He **determines** the course of the conversation. He says what's going to be done. And he does the kissing. Not us, just him. But maybe it would be different if Paul and I hadn't kissed before. With that tingling feeling running through our bodies, utterly in love. I don't think Lubo's in love with me. He's just trying

---

what the hell! – was soll's!; to clench – klemmen;
reed – Schilfgras; surface – Oberfläche;
to determine – bestimmen

his luck, maybe it'll work. That would be OK. All the girls in school, every single one of them, even Anna, would be quite happy with that. A kiss is a kiss, and a kiss from Lubo is a kiss from Lubo. But for me it doesn't **count**. I love Paul. I know that now more than ever before, and that's why I don't let Lubo continue to kiss me.

"Sorry, I can't!" I try to explain to him. Wow, I'm apologising!

But Lubo doesn't listen to me. He just pulls me closer again.

And I push him away. I have no idea if anyone has ever done this to him before, except his parents, of course. "I'm in love with someone else, OK?" Straight out of the movies.

Lubo stares at me, a picture of **bewilderment**.

I look around, trying to find the best way out of the water, above all, away from Lubo. Then I spot Anna **in the clutches** of the couple who have just come back to their house. She let herself get caught, of course! And I accepted full responsibility. So see you, Lubo.

As I head towards Anna and the couple, I try to come up with a plan. I expect they've already called the police. So what can I say? And what **penalty** do people have to pay for doing something like this?

---

to count – zählen; bewilderment – Verblüffung; in the clutches – in den Fängen; penalty – Strafe

The man **austerely** folds his arms over his chest as he sees me coming out of the water. He's wearing a straw hat, and he's got loads of **laughter lines**. But he's not laughing right now. "Aha, your **backup**!" he says to Anna.

She turns around to me and looks really **relieved**. She almost manages a smile on her bright red face. I just go and stand next to her. Let's hear what they have to say.

The woman is very fat. She has two tiny brown eyes in her **chubby** face. Friendly eyes. But are they friendly right now?

"If I clean the place up, they won't call the police. That's the deal," Anna explains to me and gets a nod of **confirmation** from the man in the straw hat. "If you help me, it'll go quicker!"

Of course, I'll help her. Mrs Friendly Eyes even gives us a glass of lemonade. And I have plenty of time to tell Anna all about the kiss and about how I now know that I'm really going to miss Paul. Because I love him.

---

austere – streng; laughter lines – Lachfalten;
backup – Unterstützung; relieved – erleichtert;
chubby – pummelig; confirmation – Bestätigung

In the Fog of Paul

Bond Street. A ***gloomy*** *Saturday. A cloud of* ***fog*** *drifts along the ground, wrapping itself* ***mercilessly*** *around anything that stands in its way, like rubber. But it won't stop her. Although her legs are as heavy as* ***lead,*** *and the fog is tightening its hold on them, trying to drag her down into the depths of the* ***sewers*** *where it intends to* ***devour*** *her, she goes on, always looking ahead through her Super 8 camera, her finger on the record button. The rats* ***squeal*** *noisily, and the camera gently hums.*

ABC gave me the film as a present. They really went for it.

"Today is Sunday and we're going to the flea market," Anna **resolved**.

Carla threw me out of bed, and Babsi decided what I should wear.

"You don't need to worry about me. Just let me die in peace!"

---

gloomy – düster; fog – Nebel; merciless – gnadenlos; lead – Blei; sewers – Kanalisation; to devour – verschlingen; to squeal – quieken; to resolve – beschließen

My protest hardly made any impression on them.

After they had made me a slice of toast, buttered it, cut it up into thin pieces as if I was some **toothless** old biddy, and somehow managed to **stuff** it into my mouth, we set off.

"I can't go out on the street like this!" I moaned.

"You look sweet!"

"Being **depressed** makes you sexy. Think of Marilyn!"

"You can still go out, even if you look like shit!"

Mum has gone to Holland with her new family. Mr and Mrs Gorilla with the sweet babies and a **strapping** young man. Probably with his girlfriend. Big-breasted gorilla girl.

It goes without saying that Mum understood I didn't want to go with them. A long weekend with Paul in a small hut on the beach, absolutely idyllic, it would drive me mad! I didn't even need to explain to Mum why I didn't want to come. She just left me in peace. It's the first time I've ever been at home on my own. **Unsupervised**.

"You won't do anything stupid?" was her only warning.

"Paul isn't here," I replied and continued painting my black picture. I found it somewhere, and it wasn't black to begin with. In fact, it was a large

---

toothless – zahnlos; to stuff – stopfen; depressed – deprimiert; strapping – stattlicher; unsupervised – ohne Aufsicht

picture of a **meadow** of flowers painted with dots. Two girls in long dresses were running through the flowers hand in hand. Now it's a black picture. **Jet black**.

"Are you sure I can leave you alone?" asked Mum, concerned.

Sure. I tried to smile at her. "It's just a coincidence that it's black. It's art, know what I mean?"

A kiss on the artist's cheek, a fridge full of goodies, and the funny ape family were gone.

"I can't be bothered today!" I continued to moan in the **tram**, but there was no point.

"You can't seriously think that we would leave you at home alone in your condition?" Anna's eyes filled with tears. "Are we friends or not?" She held out her hand, wanting us to put our hands on top of hers and look deep into each others eyes and **swear** eternal friendship.

But, of course, we didn't do it – it's silly – we can do without that.

Anna just took both of my hands and squeezed them tightly. "We're friends. Forever!"

Babsi and Carla rolled their eyes. With good reason. After all, they **left us in the lurch** when we were with Lubo. Guilty conscience **justified**.

---

meadow – Wiese; jet black – pechschwarz; tram – Straßenbahn; to swear – schwören; to leave sb in the lurch – jmdn. im Stich lassen; justified – berechtigt

"How were we meant to know that you'd both **volunteer** to take the **blame**?" Babsi.

"If you let yourself be caught by such old people, then it's probably what you wanted in the first place," said Miss **PhD Psychologist** Carla.

Anna and I just looked at each other and shrugged our shoulders. It wasn't worth talking about. As a **punishment** we didn't tell them anything about the kiss.

"In any case, no one has ever got through all the horrible phases of being in love as quickly as you, Olli," claimed Carla dryly.

"Change the subject!" But quickly, please.

"Have you tried forgetting him?" asked Anna.

Babsi shook her head. "It doesn't go that quickly, Anna!"

"Yeah, but you can try it quickly!"

"I've never heard of anyone who's been able to **influence** the speed of forgetting!" Carla was probably going through all her philosophy books in her head.

"But have you, Olli?" You always have to give Anna an answer, otherwise she never lets you go. Ever.

---

to volunteer – sich freiwillig zu etw. melden; blame – Schuld; PhD Psychologist (= Doctor of Philosophy) – Doktor der Philosophie; punishment – Strafe; to influence – beeinflussen

"Look, I managed to go to Lubo's! And I've written Paul a million letters and thrown them all away. I've sorted through the entire storeroom and painted a black picture. I've even learnt the next Latin chapter **in advance**. But I haven't forgotten him!"

Anna, Babsi and Carla sigh. They can imagine what I've been through.

At the flea market I did end feeling a little bit better. Perhaps I shouldn't become a nun. Instead I could become an eccentric old lady who always pulls along a **handcart** full of old things behind her and wanders from flea market to flea market. An old flea lady, yes. Someone who sleeps in her cosy cardboard box under the bridge. Her only friends are rusty silver teapots which have been broken for years, but she's happy. Rusty old teapots can't let you down.

"Scram! It's Chorche!" Babsi tore me out of my thoughts and **dragged** me into hiding – of all places behind a stall selling second-hand trainers. "He wants his kiss!"

I immediately grasped the situation. Babsi had sold herself for me. And I was thinking about teapots!

"I was against it," said Anna, huddling next to me and holding her nose because of the trainers. "I

---

in advance – im Voraus; handcart – Leiterwagen;
to drag – schleppen

mean, that's practically prostitution, don't you think, Olli?"

Babsi grinned at me and runs her **moist** tongue **seductively** over her red lips.

I agree with Anna: "You're right. Babsi is a **tart**!"

Anna's eyes nearly pop out of her head. "How can you say something like that? She did it for you!"

Oh, come on! Then we all had to burst into laughter. I'd never have thought it would ever happen to me again. Really. Laughing, I mean.

Eventually Jorge disappeared, and we could **resurface**. We each **immersed ourselves** in other things. Anna looked at the old, embroidered clothes, reading all the phrases on them lettering like: *Cast flowers of love during your life, and keep one another from* ***strife***. Carla was **engrossed** in a bookstall with century-old books where you couldn't even read the writing, not even the title, **let alone** what was inside. All the pages were yellow, and the lettering looked like it was written by my grandma. Babsi was waving to what she considered to be gorgeous boys, and I just strolled along seeing nothing because I couldn't help thinking about Paul again.

---

moist – feucht; seductive – verführerisch; tart (ugs.) – Nutte;
to resurface – wieder auftauchen;
to immerse oneself in sth – sich in etw. vertiefen; strife – Konflikt; engrossed – vertieft; let alone – geschweige denn

What was he doing right now with Linda on the beach? Hand in hand, the wind blowing in their hair, **defying** everything that could stand against them from outside – including mad, **flat-chested** girls who **got** strange **things into their heads**. They've probably slipped off their shoes and were running to and fro from the waves, looking a bit stupid. In the end they'll fall into the sand and give in to the **long awaited** kiss.

"Olli, hello, we're here!" ABC tore me out of my thoughts. They were standing in front of me with a grin on their faces because they'd just bought the cups. The mother-of-pearl cups.

"They'd gone down in price!" Anna quickly informed me.

"No one wanted them apart from you. And rightly so!" Contempt from Carla.

"You old flea lady!" said Babsi, putting her arm around my shoulders and pointing into one of the cups. There was a Super 8 film inside. "We thought you could make a little film about it. You know, the thing with Paul!"

"You can make a film and **unburden** your heart. And then maybe you can forget it. Right, Carla?"

Carla nodded grimly. "It's worth a try!"

---

to defy – trotzen; flat-chested – flachbrüstig;
to get sth into your head – sich etw. einbilden;
long awaited – lang ersehnt; to unburden – abladen

Bond Street. She's finally made it. Having drawn on all her strength, she's managed to drag herself to his house. She stands on the other side of the street and films. Films the scene of horror. The place where he once **cast a spell over** *her with his tentative,* **reticent** *kiss, only then to use her, suck the life out of her, and* **torture** *her until the bitter end.*

The fog slowly creeps up her legs, slipping into her trouser legs, seeping into every pore of her skin. The house is dark. The birds have flown away in search of fresh **prey**. *She's of no interest to them. She's empty,* **burnt-out**, *a shadow of her former self. And although she knows all this, although she saw through the blood-sucking* **machinations** *of this family, there's nothing more she wants than to go to them, to be with them. She's drawn to this horrible house as if* **possessed**. *She now takes the first step towards that house, desperately fighting the fog, but she won't make it. She's got no strength left. The fog is stronger. It drags her down into the depths.*

---

to cast a spell over sb – jmdn. in seinen Bann ziehen;
reticent – zurückhaltend; to torture – foltern;
prey – Opfer/Beute; burnt-out – verbraucht;
machinations – Machenschaften; possessed – besessen

ABC at the Flea Market

ABC are sitting on a fence next to the **snack bar**, looking like chickens in a roost. Babsi on the left, Carla on the right, Anna in the middle.

"She went there. Without us!" sighs Anna, lost in thought. She stares into the distance as if she were hoping to spot the last trace of Olli. But that's out of the question because Olli left over half an hour ago.

"We can't leave her all alone at home this evening," says Babsi, thinking aloud. "I bet she'll spend the whole time thinking about what Paul is doing in Holland with Linda, and what her mum's doing with gorilla. Just the thought makes me feel sick."

"Maybe we should **call around** and make her something to eat? Something light but tasty," suggests Anna. "It might **take her mind off** things."

"We could bring a few boys with us …!" That was Babsi, of course.

---

snack bar – Imbissstube; to call around – vorbeischauen; to take sb's mind off sth – jmdn. von etw. ablenken

Now Carla's had enough. "Leave her in peace. We've only just given her the film to use. How is she meant to do that if we don't give her any time?"

"It would be better if we made the film together anyway," thinks Anna.

But Carla shakes her head. "Olli needs time for herself, even if it's a bit hard for us."

"And what if it's only you who thinks that," objects Babsi, "and **in reality** she spends the whole evening **mentally** begging us to turn up and comfort Olli?"

"Did the whole thing with Paul go as I **predicted** or not?" Carla is irritated.

Anna and Babsi have to admit she's right. Carla had predicted the whole disaster from the very beginning.

"Are men **beasts**?"

Anna and Babsi nod.

But then Anna thinks twice, "Maybe that's a bit of a sweeping **generalisation** ...!"

All of a sudden, Babsi gets all **flustered**. She ducks down and **prods** the others. "Talking of beasts, look who's standing at the snack bar!"

Paul. As clear as day.

---

in reality – in Wirklichkeit; mentally – in Gedanken; to predict sth – etw. voraussagen; beast – Monster/(hier:) Schwein; generalisation – Verallgemeinerung; flustered – aufgeregt; to prod sb – jmdn. stoßen

"Hey, why isn't he in Holland?" whispers Anna.

Babsi jumps down from the fence. "He can tell us himself!"

Paul is waiting in the never-ending **queue** in front of the snack bar and is so **preoccupied with** himself that he only notices the three girls when they plant themselves in front of him, arms folded, their faces grim, **fiercely resolute**.

Paul is **startled**. He looks from one girl to the next.

"You don't know us, but we know you," explains Carla, "and that's why we'd really like to know why you're not in Holland."

"You … you really hurt Olli …!" Anna, honest as ever.

Babsi digs her elbow into Anna's side and looks at her reproachfully.

"Ouch, are you crazy?"

"Olli's doing great," says Babsi, trying to **rescue** the situation. "But we still want to know why you aren't in Holland."

Paul looks at the three girls as if they were **off their trolley**. "Who are you? Who wants to know?"

---

queue – Schlange; to be preoccupied with sth – sich mit etw. stark beschäftigen;
fiercely resolute – wild entschlossen;
to be startled – erschreckt/überrascht; to rescue – retten;
to be off one's trolley – nicht mehr ganz dicht sein

"We're Olli's protectors!" Babsi declares.

"The **guardians** of her heart!" stresses Anna theatrically.

"Just friends!" qualifies Carla.

Paul nods slowly as if he was gradually beginning to understand. Then his turn comes up to order a sausage. "Do any of you want something?" he asks the girls.

"You don't actually think you can **bribe** us?" retorts Anna, full of **indignation**.

"Over my dead body!" hisses Babsi.

"A small portion of chips for me," chirps Carla and receives a look of contempt from her **uncompromising comrades-in-arms**.

They sit down at a beer table where the traces of the four million other people who have already eaten their sausage there today can still be seen. Paul on one side, the three girls on the other.

"I'm not in Holland," says Paul, cutting his sausage into small pieces, "because I couldn't hack being in a romantic hut by the seaside with Olli!"

"You wouldn't be able to resist each other, huh?" says Babsi, raising an eyebrow.

Paul shrugs his shoulders. "That's not it."

"Linda won't let you go, right?" speculates Anna.

---

guardian – Wächter; to bribe – bestechen;
indignation – Entrüstung; uncompromising – kompromisslos;
comrade-in-arms – Kriegskamerad

Paul looks at her suspiciously. "You know everything!"

Carla eats her chips and nods.

Paul smiles wistfully. "Linda wouldn't mind. We're not together anymore. I told Olli that already. I didn't go because Olli has a boyfriend, and I just can't bear it. OK?"

Anna jumps up. "You're lying!" she declares, utterly outraged. "Why did you and Linda **snog** in the church then?"

"You'd only just found out that Olli was taken, and you jumped right back into Linda's arms!" shrieks Babsi.

"Men!" mutters Carla as cool as a cucumber with her mouth full.

Paul shakes his head, **daubing** his chips stick in his ketchup. "Linda and I don't snog anymore! She might have congratulated me because we performed well ..." He **falters** and stares at the girls. "Who says they saw it?"

ABC look at each other. Can we say? And who's telling the truth? Can it all have been just one big misunderstanding?

Carla **swallows**. "Olli. Olli saw you both. She wanted to tell you that Chorche wasn't her boyfriend and that she really ...!"

---

to snog – [rum]knutschen; to daub sth – etw. beschmieren; to falter – stocken; to swallow – schlucken

Babsi interrupts her before Carla goes too far and even mentions the word love. Don't ever give up your dignity. "… that she really thinks you're OK!"

Anna grabs Paul by the sleeve, her feelings **gushing over**. "… that she loves you. Like crazy!"

Just then Jorge comes rushing up from behind, grabs Babsi, turns her around to him, whispers, "*Tesoro*, I love you, only you!" and kisses her right on the mouth. **Passionately** and with lots of you-know-what.

Babsi tries to defend herself and **wriggle free**, not wanting this to be happening, but Jorge won't let her go, and eventually she stops wriggling.

Carla rolls her eyes, and Anna looks away.

Paul doesn't understand a thing anymore. He has the sneaking suspicion that things aren't quite as they seem with Olli's boyfriend, but otherwise he **remains in the dark**. What chaos! He gets to his feet and is about to go. "Right then," he sighs. "Everything's cleared up then!"

Anna and Carla stare at him as he goes. Then Anna jumps up and runs after him. Carla remains seated, finishing off her chips before they go cold.

"You can't actually be serious," Anna shouts. "Now wait a minute!"

---

to gush over – überkochen; passionate – leidenschaftlich;
to wriggle free – sich befreien;
to remain in the dark – keine Ahnung haben

Paul turns around to her. "It's all a complete **mess**. Olli won't believe a word I say, and I haven't got the foggiest idea what's going on!"

Anna stops right in front of him, practically nose to nose, and puts on her face of **conviction**. It looks like this: her cheeks start to **flush**, gradually her whole face turns red, and she stares at the person opposite her with a **penetrating** gaze as if she were trying to hypnotise him. "And so that's it, huh? This is meant to be Prince Charming Paul who Olli always told us about?"

Carla watches on from the table with a grin on her face. To the left Anna is trying to talk some sense into Paul, to her right Babsi is kissing Jorge, and she's sitting in the middle stuffing her face with chips. She shakes her head and makes a noise like a horse. "Where is it all going to end?"

---

to be a mess – total verkorkst sein; conviction – Überzeugung; to flush – erröten; penetrating – durchdringend

Friends at last

So. Now I've used half the film to **come to terms** with Bond Street. What now? Nothing's changed. It's just made me feel even worse. I escape from Paul's fog and go home. That's better. I hope. No, I'll make it better, for myself. I'll arrange a room for mourning.

The things you need for a mourning room:
1 TV
1 sofa
3 blankets (at least)
1 **remote control**
(so you don't have to move at all)
Malt beer (unlimited) and/or peppermint tea
(so that mourning hurts, real bad)
A small **assortment** of salty food: olives, peanuts, sandwiches with cheese and/or salami
A **considerably** larger assortment of sweet food: chocolate of all sorts (dark chocolate suits the

---

to come to terms with sth – sich mit etw. abfinden;
remote control – Fernbedienung; assortment – Auswahl;
considerable – deutlich

mood best of all), **blancmange**, sweeties, all existing chocolate bars in mini-size, **Sugar Puffs** (without milk), etc.
1 telephone for emergency calls

Wearing a baggy T-shirt and baggy **tracksuit bottoms**, I **barricade myself in** under the three blankets and pull them up under my nose. From there I **peer out** at the TV and start channel-hopping. A romantic movie from the **year dot**; a flirt show; a talk show on the topic *he loves me – he loves me not*; a modern romantic movie … It's driving me crazy. They usually just show quiz shows – question after question on every channel – and today? Love all over the place. Is it World Love Day or something? Hello, I'd know about that. I would have noticed it one way or another.

I decide to watch a programme showing poor, tortured animals which **viewers** can take home with them to **shower with love**. I think about Paul. The two of us going through the skip refuse. I've never had such a nice time with anyone going through skip refuse before. The worst thing about

---

blancmange – Pudding; Sugar Puffs™ – Honigpops; tracksuit bottoms – Trainingshose; to barricade oneself in – sich hinter etw. verschanzen; to peer out – spähen; in the year dot – Anno dazumal; viewer – Fernsehzuschauer; to shower with love – mit Liebe überschütten

the whole thing is that it could have worked out perfectly. Even the obstacle of Linda was out of the way. But now? Now I can't go to him and say, "Look, Paul, would you mind dumping Linda again? I mean, for real this time?" I **blew it**. It's as simple as that. It was just one big cock-up. That's it with love for me. It's over with Paul. For good!

A huge dog is looking at me out of the television. His eyes are so incredibly sad that I just have to start crying. He's looking right at me! He needs me! Maybe that's the best solution: instead of becoming a nun or a flea lady, I could become a dog-rescuer. That's a **lifelong task**. Children on the street would watch me pass with open mouths and call out to each other, "Look, there's the dog lady!" when I **go for walkies** with my seventeen dogs. Dogs are **faithful**. Dogs really love. ONLY dogs really love. Rubbish!

I expect they're making some weird cheese fondue on the beach in Holland right now. The whole family. And if someone drops something in it, he has to kiss the person to his left. To Paul's left is Linda. And he **deliberately** keeps dropping his dip, just so he can kiss her. That's what they're doing. The left and right hand of the devil keep poking each other's eyes out with their fondue forks. No

---

to blow it – etw. versauen; lifelong task – Lebensaufgabe; to go walkies – Gassi gehen; faithful – treu; deliberate – absichtlich

one notices because they're all too busy dropping their dips in the cheese. After dinner everybody's unbelievably **full**, and they have to go on a lovely walk because there's nothing else to do in Holland but stroll along the beach. They lead the blind brats along and laugh into the wind. Really, I'm so happy I'm not there.

The dog show is finally over, but now there's football. That's bad, but still better than some stupid romantic movie. I stare blankly at the **box**, stuffing my face with Sugar Puffs and washing them down with a malt beer. Perverse! Maybe it would have been better if ABC had **come to my aid**. A big pile of mattresses in front of the TV. The whole night long. I expect we would have kept on talking about Paul. Again and again. How unbearable! But on the other hand …

The doorbell rings.

I remain **motionless** under my layer of blankets. Who could it be? The girls? No. I told them not to come, so it wouldn't be them. It's probably someone who wants to dump old newspapers in our letter boxes. But I'm not getting up, you can forget it.

The doorbell rings again.

He's pretty pushy, this newspaper guy. He must

---

full – satt; box – Glotze;
to come to the aid of sb – jmdm. zu Hilfe kommen;
motionless – bewegungslos

be crazy, it's Sunday! And what if it is the girls? No, I'm not getting up. I want to be alone in my mourning room. I pull the blankets over my head and disappear into the darkness, probably because I think I won't hear anything there. I know I'm being stupid.

The doorbell rings again. Twice **in a row**.

OK, it's the girls. Maybe they're worried about me and think I've put a **bullet** through my head or have started a hunger strike or something. They just want to check up on me, and I won't even open the door. **Outrageous**.

I slowly get up and shuffle in slow motion to the door, like an old grandma. Then I press the automatic door-opener for downstairs and shuffle back under my protective blankets.

They come in, close the front door and come into the sitting room. The mourning room.

"It's good you're here. It's a really exciting **match**!" They don't need to know that I've spent the whole time thinking about Paul.

"Really? I don't know anything about football!"

But it's not the girls. It's not the newspaper guy either. It's Paul! I immediately shoot up and turn around. He's standing there, flesh and blood, grinning in the middle of my mourning room.

---

in a row – hintereinander; bullet – Kugel; outrageous – unmöglich; match – Spiel

"Er … what … why aren't you in Holland?"

"Strange. That seems to be the question of the day! – May I?" He points at Mum's well **worn** armchair.

Of course, he can. Even though I don't understand anything right now. All of a sudden, I remember that I'm wearing my baggy tracksuit bottoms and an even baggier T-shirt. I look like I weigh two tonnes and have never heard the word 'waist' before. And what's more, I've been crying, because of the dog just now, and, oh God, I must look absolutely terrible.

"May I?" I mumble and disappear under my pile of blankets.

"Nice stuff you've got here," I hear Paul say from outside the blanket world.

"Help yourself!" I say a bit louder than normal so that he can understand me.

I hear him chewing. It sounds like Sugar Puffs. "Wouldn't you rather come out from under those blankets?" asks Paul cautiously.

I shake my head dramatically so that he can make out what I mean from outside the blanket world. "No way. I look like … like … I can't!"

"I think you look pretty good."

Did he just say that? Did I just hear that? What is he doing here anyway? What about the cheese

---

worn – abgewetzt

fondue? I pull back the blankets and look at him. "What are you doing here anyway?"

Paul doesn't say anything. He just gets to his feet and disappears into the corridor. Then he comes back in with our umbrella **skeleton**. And there are loads of photos hanging from it. "I made you the photo stand you wanted."

I can't believe my eyes. How sweet, how utterly sweet! I forget the fact that I'm wearing my baggy tracksuit bottoms and an even baggier T-shirt, and I don't shuffle like a grandma but rush over to the work of art and look at the photos.

"They're pictures of Bond Street. Of the parts where … you know … where …!"

"… where the skip refuse was!" I help him out and beam at him. "Great!" I can't get anymore out.

Paul fiddles with his **fingernails**. "It was all a misunderstanding. I … I've been thinking about you ever since … ever since the kiss. No, actually since the family get-together and the chaos with Fritz and Franz. But then that guy came along …"

"That was a misunderstanding," I interrupt him. "He doesn't exist!"

Now we're standing there, the umbrella between us – the **object** with which it all began – and we don't know what to say. It's obvious to us both that

---

skeleton – Skelett; fingernail – Fingernagel;
object – Gegenstand

there's nothing more to explain. It was all just a big misunderstanding.

Paul grins. "Yeah, the guy who I thought was together with you ... he's now together with your friend."

"Chorche? No, that can't be." I sit down on the sofa and have to laugh. What makes him think that?

"When I left the flea market they were still kissing with everything they had."

"Babsi and Chorche?" I can't believe it.

"Well, you know, the one who tries to look like Marilyn Monroe."

Babsi and Jorge.

"With their you-know-what?" I can't resist asking.

"Their I-know-what?"

I grin and wave my hand at Paul, shaking my head **in disbelief**. I keep on shaking my head because I can't think of anything more to say. One thing's for sure: I don't want to talk about French kissing with Paul.

"May I?" Paul sits down next to me.

I **shove over** a bit to make room for him, and he puts his arm around me. Just like that. I get an electric shock. I freeze. I'm **as stiff as a poker**.

---

in disbelief – ungläubig; to shove over – rutschen; as stiff as a poker – stocksteif

Paul **pinches** me lightly. “Look at me!”

When he says those words there’s nothing I can do but look at him, we know that by now. I look at him, right into his eyes, and he kisses me, right on my mouth.

Someone scores a goal on the television, and the people in the stadium start **cheering**, “’aulandolli, ’aulandolli, ’aulandolli!”

Hold on, that’s not the television! Paul and I shoot **apart**.

The left and right hand of the devil are charging around the sofa.

Mum and Robert are standing in the doorway, smiling dreamily. “Oh, sorry to disturb you!”

“What are you doing here?” Paul and I ask at exactly the same time. We both thought they wouldn’t be back until tomorrow – they wanted to take full advantage of every possible night together, of course.

Then comes the terrible **tale** of how the devil’s hands buried the key to the seaside hut in the sand, somewhere along the huge beach in Holland. And there was no **spare key**. Then it started to rain, and they had no other choice but to return home.

“How about me cooking us something to eat?”

---

to pinch sb – jmdn. kneifen; to cheer – jubeln;
apart – auseinander; tale – Geschichte;
spare key – Ersatzschlüssel

asks Robert and, of course, no one has anything against it.

Later on we all sit around the **coffee table**, eating. The football match still isn't over, and the devil's hands are trying to spit **mashed potatoes** at each other.

"Hey!" I shout at them and point my finger. "I don't want you to do that!"

They freeze in mid-motion and look at me. Is she serious? They look at Robert. He shrugs his shoulders: apparently! So they decide to eat the mashed potatoes instead, and I go and get the Super 8 camera because no one will believe this is actually happening later. I film the chaos from the stairwell leading to the storeroom. Everybody grins and freezes because they think I'm taking a photo. Then Paul stands up and comes over to me. His beautiful face gets bigger and bigger – and then the film runs out. Rat-ta-tat-tat.

"Where does that go to?" he asks, looking at the stairwell.

"Secret rooms!" I whisper.

And that's where he wants to go with me now. He takes me by the hand. Electric shock!

---

coffee table – Couchtisch; mashed potatoes – Kartoffelpüree

Von Brinx/Kömmerling bei Thienemann bereits erschienen:

Weiberalarm!
Weiberalarm Stufe rot!
Alles Hühner – außer Ruby!
So ein Larry!
Cool, cooler, sechzehn!
Alles Machos – außer Tim!
Ein Paul zum Küssen
Stadt, Land, Liebe

Brinx, Thomas/Kömmerling, Anja:
A Paul to Kiss
Aus dem Deutschen von David Fermer
ISBN 3 522 17764 9

Reihengestaltung: Birgit Schössow
Einbandillustration: Birgit Schössow
Texttypografie: Marlis Killermann
Schrift: Esprit book
Satz: KCS GmbH, Buchholz/Hamburg
Reproduktion: Medienfabrik, Möglingen
Druck und Bindung: Friedrich Pustet, Regensburg

5 4 3 2 1*   05 06 07 08

Thienemann im Internet: www.thienemann.de